W9-CLV-451

decorating
INSIDE and OUT

If you love the casual comfort and colorful charm of a garden setting, this book is for you! We've given new purpose to lawn chairs, fountains, fencing, and other patio accessories to create one-of-a-kind furnishings for every room of your house. There's even a serene home office. Whether you want to transform your home into a garden paradise or just refresh it with a few botanical motifs, you'll find inspiration here in the clever ideas and splendid color photographs. And once you've chosen a project, the step-by-step instructions ensure a successful finished product. Your family and friends will be delighted with the relaxed appeal these outdoor-inspired furnishings instill in your décor!

LEISURE ARTS, INC.
Little Rock, Arkansas

EDITORIAL STAFF

Editor-in-Chief: Anne Van Wagner Childs
Executive Director: Sandra Graham Case
Director of Designer Relations: Debra Nettles
Design Director: Cyndi Hansen
Editorial Director: Susan Frantz Wiles
Publications Director: Kristine Anderson Mertes
Creative Art Director: Gloria Bearden
Photography Director: Karen Hall
Art Operations Director: Jeff Curtis

DESIGN
Senior Designers: Anne Pulliam Stocks and Linda Diehl Tiano
Designers: Polly Tullis Browning, Cherece Athy Cooper, Jennifer Todd, and Becky Werle
Design Assistant: Debra Smith

TECHNICAL
Managing Editor: Sherry Solida Ford
Technical Writers: Leslie Schick Gorrell and Theresa Hicks Young
Copy Editor: Susan Frazier
Technical Associate: K. J. Smith
Technical Assistant: Sharon Gillam

EDITORIAL
Managing Editor: Linda L. Trimble
Associate Editors: Darla Burdette Kelsay, Alan Caudle, Suzie Puckett, and Jennifer L. Riley

ART
Art Director: Mark Hawkins
Graphic Artist: Elaine Barry
Photography Stylists: Sondra Daniel, Tiffany Huffman, Elizabeth Lackey, and Janna Laughlin
Staff Photographer: Russell Ganser
Publishing Systems Administrator: Becky Riddle
Publishing Systems Assistants: Myra S. Means and Chris Wertenberger

PROMOTIONS
Managing Editor: Alan Caudle
Associate Editor: Steven M. Cooper
Designer: Dale Rowett
Graphic Artist: Deborah Kelly

BUSINESS STAFF

Publisher: Rick Barton
Vice President, Finance: Tom Siebenmorgen
Director of Corporate Planning and Development: Laticia Mull Cornett
Vice President, Retail Marketing: Bob Humphrey
Vice President, National Accounts: Pam Stebbins

Retail Marketing Director: Margaret Sweetin
Vice President, Operations: Jim Dittrich
Distribution Director: Rob Thieme
Retail Customer Service Manager: Wanda Price
Vice President, Production and Distribution: Phillip Lee
Production Manager: Greg Amason

Copyright© 2000 by Leisure Arts, Inc., 5701 Ranch Drive, Little Rock, Arkansas 72223-9633. All rights reserved. No part of this book may be reproduced in any form or by any means without the prior written permission of the publisher, except for brief quotations in reviews appearing in magazines or newspapers. We have made every effort to ensure that these instructions are accurate and complete. We cannot, however, be responsible for human error, typographical mistakes, or variations in individual work. Made in the United States of America.

Hardcover ISBN 1-57486-188-3
Softcover ISBN 1-57486-221-9

10   9   8   7   6   5   4   3   2   1

contents

contents

inviting retreat

PERFECT FOR READING AND RELAXING

Looking for a sunny place to escape with your favorite magazine and a refreshing snack? Consider transforming a corner of the porch into your own private retreat. Start with simple furnishings dressed in natural fabrics like muslin and canvas for a light and airy look; then surround yourself with garden elements that nurture a love of nature. This collection is the fruit of an easy technique in which you stamp-paint with half a crisp pear for a pattern that's fresh and inviting. Add some scented candles and a wall vase of our carefree pinecone flowers to set a relaxing mood. A stack of vintage suitcases makes a handy side table where you can store things between visits to keep clutter to a minimum.

Inspired by a passion for pears, the luscious print on our muslin table skirt is stamped on with acrylic paint and highlighted by hand.

Want to set a relaxing mood? Dig up a couple of small garden spades, team them with aromatic candles, and you have wall-mounted sconces (opposite, top left) that will pamper you with candlelight. A flea market-found wooden box becomes a handy magazine holder (opposite, top right), cleverly decorated with seed packets and a raffia bow. Beneath it all lies a sisal throw rug, complemented with a floral fabric border.

A salvaged metal ceiling tile adds architectural interest as the roof of a gently aged birdhouse perched atop a wooden spindle.

A natural for the porch, a lightweight director's chair (opposite) is ripe with creative possibilities, and it's easy on the wallet. The removable back and seat are like blank canvases just waiting to be adorned with garden styling. We transformed one chair with our pear print, but why not paint a pair?

11

Add to the natural décor with a big bouquet of painted pinecone flowers. Ours look extra nostalgic in a cone-shaped wall vase folded from an old metal ceiling tile that we found at a flea market.

inviting retreat

PEAR PRINT TABLE COVER

Our table cover is designed to "puddle" and is photographed on a table that is 36" in diameter and 30" high. If your table is smaller, you may wish to reduce the size of your table cover accordingly.

You will need 3 yds. of 108"w muslin; thumbtack; string; fabric marking pencil; pinking shears; 10 yds. of 3" long cotton bullion fringe; fresh pear; tan, light yellow, green, and mauve acrylic paint; and paintbrushes.

1. Working on a large, flat surface, fold fabric in half from top to bottom and again from left to right. Referring to *Cutting a Fabric Circle*, page 127, use pinking shears to cut a 106" circle from fabric.

2. On right side of table cover, pin fringe along edge overlapping ends and folding under raw end. Using a wide zig-zag stitch, sew fringe in place.

3. Cut pear in half lengthwise. Paint cut side of one pear half with tan paint. With area of table cover to be stamped on a flat, protected surface, stamp with pear half. Lighten one side of stamped shape with brush strokes of yellow paint; darken remaining side with mauve. Add tan stem and green leaf. Repeat to add desired number of stamped pears to table cover, allowing paint to dry before moving to each new area to be stamped.

PINECONE FLOWERS

You will need side-cut tin snips; pinecones; wire cutters; awl; 18-gauge floral wire; hot glue gun; green floral tape; yellow, gold, rust, and burgundy acrylic paint; paintbrushes; and acrylic spray sealer.

Allow paint and sealer to dry after each application.

1. For each flower, use tin snips to cut off top half of one pinecone; discard. Use wire cutters to cut scales from cut end of cone to form a $1/4$" to $1/2$" long flower center.

2. Use awl to make a hole in bottom of flower; apply glue to one end of wire and insert in hole for stem. Wrap stem with floral tape.

3. Paint flower petals desired color; paint center yellow. Spray flower with sealer.

CEILING TILE WALL VASE

You will need a hammer, awl, square metal ceiling tile (we found our 24" tile at a flea market), craft wire, wire cutters, floral foam, preserved eucalyptus and other greenery, and *Pinecone Flowers* (this page).

1. Use hammer and awl to punch holes along sides of tile (Fig. 1). Referring to dotted lines and matching holes, fold tile to form cone. Thread 6" lengths of wire through matched holes and twist ends together inside cone to secure.

Fig. 1

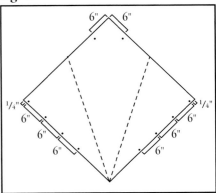

2. For hanger, thread an 18" length of wire through remaining holes at top of cone; twist ends together at back.

3. Fill cone to 3" from top with floral foam. Arrange eucalyptus, greenery and *Pinecone Flowers* in foam.

RUSTIC BIRDHOUSE WITH CEILING TILE ROOF

You will need a drill with a $1/8$" bit, wooden birdhouse, wooden spindle, wooden post top, two $1/4$" x 2" dowel screws, antique white and oxide brown acrylic paint, paste floor wax, fine sandpaper, miniature rusted fence, large rusty nail, metal ceiling tile (we found ours at a flea market), tin snips, hammer and carpet tacks.

1. Use drill and bit to drill pilot holes in center bottom of birdhouse, center of each end of spindle, and center top of post top. Using dowel screws, attach birdhouse to top of spindle and post top to bottom of spindle for base.

2. Paint birdhouse and post with brown oxide paint; allow to dry. Lightly apply floor wax to areas where paint will be sanded. Paint birdhouse and post antique white; allow to dry. Use sandpaper to remove paint from waxed areas.

3. Use household cement to attach fence to front of birdhouse. Drive rusty nail below birdhouse opening for perch.

4. Use tin snips to cut a piece from ceiling tile to fit over roof. Use carpet tacks to attach tile piece to roof.

GARDEN SPADE SCONCES

You will need two garden spades (ours measure 21" long), green acrylic paint, craft wire, wire cutters, green wired ribbon, and two green votive candles.

1. Bend each blade to form a 90° angle from handle.

2. Paint metal band on each spade green; allow to dry.

3. Wrap an 18" length of ribbon around each handle and knot at front. Trim and notch ribbon ends.

4. Thread a 6" length of wire through hole in each spade handle; twist ends together to form hanging loop.

5. Hang sconces and place candles on blades.

BORDERED SISAL RUG

You will need a 27" x 44" sisal rug; two 6" x 27" and two 6" x 44" strips of fabric, and a hot glue gun.

1. Matching wrong sides, press each fabric strip in half lengthwise, then press each long raw edge $1/2$" to wrong side. Press ends of short fabric strips to center fold to form points (Fig. 1).

Fig. 1

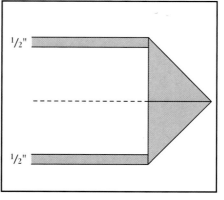

2. Inserting edges of rug into folds of each strip, glue long, then short strips to corresponding edges of rug.

DIRECTOR'S CHAIR

You will need a director's chair with removable back and seat fabric panels; fresh pear; tan, light yellow, green, and mauve acrylic paint; and paintbrushes.

1. Remove back and seat panels from chair frame.

2. Cut pear in half lengthwise. Paint cut side of one pear half with tan paint. With each panel on a flat, protected surface, stamp with pear half. Lighten one side of stamped shape with brush strokes of yellow paint; darken remaining side with mauve. Add tan stem and green leaf. Repeat to add desired number of stamped pears to panels; allow paint to dry.

3. Reassemble chair.

PLANTER BOX MAGAZINE CARRIER

You will need a wooden box with handle (we found ours at a flea market), seed packets, craft glue, and raffia.

1. Cut fronts from seed packets; glue to front of box.

2. Place several strands of raffia together; tie into a bow around box handle.

DESIGNER TIPS

Our designers offer the following suggestions for bringing an outdoor look into your home.

1. Look at your outdoor furniture with new eyes. Apply a new coat of paint or just clean up with soap and water and bring indoors.

2. Use fresh flowers or greenery from your shrubs in vases. Plant grass in baskets or shallow containers to keep summer alive.

3. Use colors like sunny yellow on walls for a feeling of bringing sunshine inside.

4. Paint a ceiling sky blue with fluffy clouds.

5. Use large floral print fabric on furniture.

6. Hang a porch swing in the corner of your room and fill with plump pillows.

7. Hang an old weathered board as a shelf and line with birdhouses.

8. Use a glass top on a birdbath as a table in a small eating area.

9. Bring a picnic table indoors and cover with a vintage tablecloth.

10. Paint terra-cotta flowerpots to use on a vanity for storing rolled-up hand towels and bath supplies.

11. Place planted window boxes in windows in an entry hall.

12. Hinge doors together for a screen or room divider.

13. Use an old watering can to hold fresh flowers.

14. Paint a metal trash can to use as a table base.

15. Paint redwood outdoor chairs in bright colors and fill with plump floral pillows.

16. Fill a glass bowl with small, smooth stones painted in soft yellows, greens, and blues.

17. Stack picnic baskets for an accent table next to a favorite chair.

18. Tie bundles of dried flowers with ribbons and hang from a curtain rod or a length cut from a slim tree branch.

19. Use a section of porch railing flanked with columns as a headboard.

20. Use a section cut from a log as a table base.

21. Place a garden bench at the foot of your bed.

22. Flank a fireplace with a pair of outdoor statues or urns placed on the hearth.

23. Keep window treatments simple to let more of the outdoors come inside.

24. Use a tabletop fountain to bring the sounds of a babbling brook inside.

25. Use framed botanical prints as artwork in unexpected places like bathrooms or even a laundry room.

delightful den

A NATURAL SETTING FOR QUIET PURSUITS

Surround yourself with serenity while relaxing in the pleasant comfort of a room designed for quiet pursuits. Candles cast a gracious glow across the outdoor-inspired décor, which is easily achieved after a visit to the local garden center. Warm colors and beautiful botanicals make this a natural setting for reading or chatting with friends.

Our fireplace screen is cleverly crafted from hinged sections of surveyor stakes that we painted white and nailed to braces. Artwork in simple wooden frames adorns the screen.

A framed letter (above) graced with a solitary feather brings to mind days of old when quills were the writing tools of choice. The weathered frame adds ambience to this unique display. Pillar candles are quickly dressed up using dried fern fronds and raffia, then set in shallow clay flowerpots. Dried bay leaves surround the votive cup.

Hanging from its stand on high, a wire birdcage (left) adds charm with its bounty of dried flowers and twist of grapevine. The small end table is an attractive accessory, painted pale green and embellished with cut lengths of twigs.

Eye-catching candleholders (right) are easy to make with fresh artichokes perched in terra-cotta flowerpots.

Timeless moss topiaries (below) standing in painted wire baskets are set atop a fringed raffia cloth scarf (also shown on page 17) on the mantel. Dried fern fronds, a sprinkling of hydrangea blossoms, and toppers of wooden turnings are the finishing touches.

Stenciled with leafy shadows, a refurbished wooden lawn chair (opposite) is the perfect place for reading or resting, with its coordinating fabric-covered cushion. Our outdoor theme continues with a classic lampshade creatively trimmed with preserved skeleton leaves pressed on textured paper.

delightful den

MANTEL SCARF
You will need ⁵/₈ yd. of 27"w raffia cloth and ⁷/₈ yd. each of 2"w cotton fringe and ³/₄"w flat trim.

1. Cut a 22" length of raffia cloth. Fold one short edge ¹/₂" to wrong side; fold ¹/₂" to wrong side again and stitch in place.

2. Cut a 27¹/₂" length of each trim. Folding trim ends ¹/₄" to wrong side, use a zigzag stitch to stitch fringe, then flat trim, along raw edge of raffia cloth.

ARTICHOKE CANDLEHOLDERS
For each candleholder, you will need floral foam, 3" dia. terra cotta flowerpot hot glue gun, fresh artichoke, craft picks, sheet moss, dried fern fronds, and a candle.

1. Cut a piece of foam to fit in pot; glue in place. Cut an opening in center of foam to fit artichoke stem.

2. Cut a 1" deep hole in top of artichoke to fit candle. Glue artichoke stem into opening in foam; secure with craft picks. Cover surface of foam with moss; glue to secure.

3. Glue pieces of fern around rim of pot.

4. Place candle in hole in top of artichoke; glue to secure.

PILLAR CANDLES
You will need spray adhesive, dried fern fronds, tall column candles, raffia, and a clay flowerpot.

1. Apply spray adhesive to wrong sides of fern fronds; carefully adhere fronds to candles.

2. If desired, wrap base of candle with raffia; knot ends to secure.

VOTIVE CANDLE CUPS
You will need a hot glue gun, dried bay leaves, votive candle cups, and strands of raffia.

1. Overlapping edges, glue bay leaves around outside of candle cups.

2. Knot strands of raffia around cups over leaves.

CANDLE CENTERPIECE
You will need a 4¹/₂" dia. and an 8" dia. clay saucer, hot glue gun, 4" square column candle, sheet moss, artificial and dried florals (we used hydrangea, Queen Anne's lace, flax grass, and grape leaves), and small artificial pears.

1. Center small saucer, upside down, in large saucer; glue in place. Place candle on small saucer.

2. Fill in saucer around candle with moss, covering rim.

3. Arrange florals and pears around candle and glue in place.

TOPIARIES
You will need cream spray paint, cream and red acrylic paint, paintbrushes, 5¹/₂" dia. wire baskets, small wooden turnings, floral foam, hot glue gun, sheet moss, craft glue, assorted plastic foam balls and cones, twigs, and assorted dried florals (we used fern fronds and hydrangeas).

1. For each topiary, spray paint basket; allow to dry. Paint wooden turning red, then cream; allow to dry.

2. Cut a 3" block of floral foam; glue in basket. Fill basket with moss to cover foam; use craft glue to secure.

3. Use craft glue to glue moss to foam shapes, covering completely; allow to dry.

4. Use lengths of several twigs to connect shapes to form topiary. Insert trunk into foam block; hot glue to secure.

5. Arrange and hot glue dried florals, twigs, and turning on topiary as desired.

TWIG-TRIMMED TABLE
You will need green acrylic paint, foam brush, small unfinished table with drawer, utility knife, twigs, hot glue gun, hammer, and small nails.

1. Paint table green; allow to dry.

2. Referring to photo, use utility knife to cut lengths of twigs to fit front and top of table and front of drawer.

3. Glue, then nail twigs in place.

FRAMED LETTER WITH STAND
You will need poster board, color photocopy of old letter, wooden frame, spray adhesive, wood tone spray, sandpaper, tack cloth, cream and green acrylic paint, paintbrushes, paste wax, hot glue gun, feather, utility knife, twigs, and raffia.

1. Cut poster board and letter to fit frame opening. Use spray adhesive to attach letter to poster board. Spray letter with wood tone spray; allow to dry.

2. Paint frame green; allow to dry. Lightly apply wax to frame. Paint frame cream; allow to dry. Sand frame lightly; wipe with tack cloth. Mount letter in frame. Center feather diagonally on letter and glue in place.

3. Referring to Fig 1, use hot glue and raffia to assemble twigs to make stand.

Fig. 1

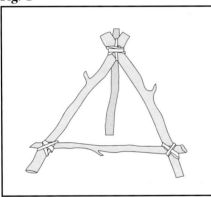

LEAFY LAMPSHADE
You will need a self-adhesive lampshade, handmade or textured paper, waxed paper, preserved skeleton leaves, and spray adhesive.

1. Follow lampshade manufacturer's instructions to cover shade with handmade or textured paper.

2. Apply spray adhesive to wrong sides of leaves; use waxed paper to carefully press leaves in place on shade.

FIREPLACE SCREEN
You will need surveyor stakes (we purchased a bundle of 1^1/$_2$"w x 36"h stakes at a home supply store), handsaw, cream and green acrylic paint, paintbrushes, hammer, 1^1/$_4$" nails, four 2^1/$_2$" long narrow utility hinges, screwdriver, three 5" x 7" unfinished wooden picture frames with hangers, and artwork for frames.

1. For braces, cut two 31" and four 14" lengths from stakes. Paint braces and remaining stakes cream; allow to dry.

2. Referring to Fig. 1 and using seventeen stakes for center section and seven stakes for each side section, use hammer and nails to assemble one center and two side sections of screen.

Fig. 1

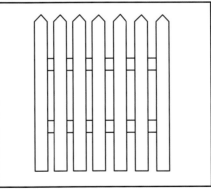

3. Position center section between side sections and mark positions for hinges. Use screwdriver to attach hinges to connect sections.

4. Paint picture frames green; allow to dry. Mount artwork in frames and attach hangers.

5. Use nails to hang frames on screen.

LEAFY STENCILED CHAIR
You will need a ready-to-finish chair (we used an Adirondack chair), light green spray paint, black permanent fine-point pen, stencil plastic, craft knife, cutting mat, green acrylic paint, a stencil brush, pillow to fit chair seat, and fabric.

1. Spray paint chair light green; allow to dry.

2. Use pattern, page 116, and follow *Stenciling*, page 127, to stencil green leaves on chair; allow to dry.

3. Measure width and length of pillow; add 1" to each measurement. Multiply width measurement by two; cut a piece of fabric the determined measurements.

4. Matching right sides and short edges, fold fabric piece in half. Leaving a long opening for turning and inserting pillow, use a ^{1}/$_2$" seam allowance to stitch raw edges together. Clip corners, turn right side out and press. Insert pillow; sew opening closed.

BIRDCAGE PLANT STAND
You will need a hanging birdcage with stand, cream spray paint, green acrylic paint, small sponge piece, 12" dia. grapevine wreath, floral wire, and wire cutters.

1. Spray paint birdcage cream; allow to dry.

2. Refer to *Painting Basics*, page 127, to *Sponge Paint* bases of birdcage and stand green.

3. Use wire cutters to cut binding from wreath and unwind; use lengths of floral wire to attach one end to top of stand. Arrange vine around stand.

airy living room

PATIO FURNITURE FRESHENS ROOM

Bring the casual comfort of a patio into the home with this airy ensemble of transformed outdoor furniture, natural accents and garden delights. From the settee and garden-trellis shelves to the birdbath arrangement and planter table, colors and accessories blend for a fresh, fun, outdoor decor ... indoors!

Set the mood with a well-dressed settee (opposite), graced with a ruffled cushion in coordinating floral print fabrics.

A garden hand rake makes an innovative photo display (below) for pictures of loved ones, while additional photographs are enclosed in frames easily decorated with twigs and dried sisal leaves.

This unique table (opposite) blends perfectly with our outdoor theme. Created using a faux terra-cotta pot with wooden and glass tabletops, the delightful decorating idea is as useful as it is pleasing to the eye. The accompanying twig basket handily holds magazines while maintaining the natural garden look of the room.

A picture frame and a clock covered with dried ammobium blossoms are lovely additions to the décor. Meanwhile, larkspur and sierra bud are the focal point of an eye-catching topiary, arrayed with beautiful nigella flowers and standing tall in a simple clay pot.

29

Our tea cart (opposite) displays a mosaic of colorful pieces of tile and broken china, while the easily crafted lamp reflects a woodsy look with its mosses, ferns, bird nest, and fabric shade, covered to match the settee cushions.

The simple beauty of dried wheat (left) adds natural appeal, whether trimmed and mounded in a clay pot, shaped into an attractive topiary, or arranged in a twig vase, as shown on page 35.

Painted terra-cotta pots (below) bloom with flowers that echo the colors in the room.

Old-fashioned botanical prints (opposite, top) displayed on slate and hung with wired ribbon are the perfect companions to an elegant square wreath of dried sisal leaves.

Relaxing is easy with lots of plump matching pillows (opposite, bottom), some with photo-transfer flowers.

A charming birdbath arrangement (left and on page 36) adds enchantment with its classic appeal and arching sprays of natural florals. Simple sheer curtains, sprinkled with tiny dried bouquets, quietly add beauty to the alluring ambience.

A garden trellis (right) looks right at home in this room. With some paint and imagination, it easily becomes an endearing indoor display featuring "knickknack" shelves and handy pegs for hanging the gardener's accessories.

It's so easy to while away the day in our peaceful "patio" room, especially in the wooden rocker (opposite), creatively painted and ready for a restful repose.

airy living room

TERRA COTTA AND GLASS TABLE

You will need eleven knob-shaped and eleven ball-shaped wooden turnings, household cement, 23" dia. round wooden tabletop with beveled edge, white and red acrylic paint, paintbrushes, white-washed faux terra cotta pot (ours measures 20" across and 16" high), self-adhesive clear vinyl glass protector dots, and a 30" dia. glass tabletop.

Allow cement and paint to dry after each application.

1. Alternating shapes and spacing evenly, use cement to attach turnings to bottom edge of wooden tabletop.

2. Thin white paint with an equal amount of water; paint wooden tabletop. Paint top surface only red. Paint over red with thinned white paint; wipe off excess.

3. To complete table base, center painted tabletop on bottom of flowerpot; use cement to glue in place.

4. Follow manufacturer's instructions to apply vinyl protector dots to glass tabletop; center tabletop on base.

TRELLIS WITH SHELVES

You will need white spray paint, wooden trellis (ours measures 22" x 72"), two 11" wide wooden shelves, 23" long wooden coat rack with wooden pegs, drill, and $1^1/4$" and $1^5/8$" wood screws.

1. Paint all wooden pieces and allow to dry; sand lightly.

2. Working from back of trellis, use wood screws and drill to attach shelves and coat rack to front of trellis.

WELL-DRESSED SETTEE

You will need a metal lawn settee, 2" thick foam, fabrics for cushion and ruffle (we used a selection of manufacturer-coordinated home decorator fabrics), and thread to match.

1. For cushion, measure width and length of settee seat; cut foam to fit. For top and bottom covers, cut two pieces of fabric $1^1/2$" larger on all sides than foam.

2. Measure height from seat to floor; add $2^1/2$". For front ruffle, cut a piece of fabric the determined height and twice as long as cushion front. For end ruffles, cut two pieces of fabric the determined height and twice as long as one end of the cushion.

3. Press short edges and one long edge of each ruffle piece 1" to wrong side; press 1" to wrong side again and stitch in place.

4. To gather remaining edge of each ruffle piece, baste $1/4$" and $3/8$ from raw edge. Pulling threads, gather each piece to fit corresponding edge of cushion.

5. Matching right sides and raw edges, center and pin ruffles on front and ends of cushion top fabric piece. Place cushion top and bottom fabric pieces right sides together. Using a $1/2$" seam allowance and leaving a long opening at back to insert foam, sew pieces together. Clip corners, turn right side out and press. Insert foam and sew opening closed.

LARGE PILLOWS

For each pillow, you will need $1^5/8$ yds. of 44"w fabric, matching thread, and a 20" square pillow form.

1. Cut two 21" squares from fabric for pillow front and back. Piecing as necessary, cut a 7" x 160" fabric piece for ruffle.

2. Matching right sides, sew ends of ruffle piece together to form a circle. Matching wrong sides and raw edges, fold ruffle piece in half lengthwise. To gather ruffle, baste $1/4$" and $3/8$" from raw edges; pull thread, drawing up gathers to fit pillow front.

3. Matching raw edges, baste ruffle to right side of pillow front. Place pillow front and back right sides together. Leaving an opening for turning, use a $1/2$" seam allowance to sew front and back together; clip corners, turn right side out and press. Insert pillow form; sew opening closed.

FLOWER TRANSFER PILLOWS

You will need fabrics (we used a selection of manufacturer-coordinated home decorator fabrics), floral images to transfer (ours are from purchased decoupage paper), photo transfer paper, sewing thread, $3/4$"w paper-backed fusible web tape, paper-backed fusible web, and polyester fiberfill.

Referring to transfer paper manufacturer's instructions, have desired image for each pillow copied onto transfer paper at a copy shop. For best results, use a solid, light-colored fabric for area of pillow where transfer will be placed. Use a $1/2$" seam allowance for all sewing unless indicated otherwise.

Envelope Pillow

1. Cut two 15" squares from fabric for pillow front and back.

2. Cut two 10" x 15" rectangles from fabric; place right sides together. Referring to Fig. 1, draw lines from center bottom of rectangles to upper corners. Cut on lines to make triangles for pillow envelope flap.

Fig. 1

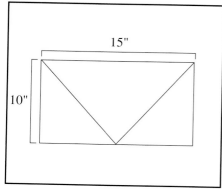

3. Matching right sides, sew point edges of flap together; clip point, turn right side out and press. Follow manufacturer's instructions to transfer floral image to one side of pillow flap.

4. Matching right sides and raw edges, place pillow flap between pillow front and back fabric squares. Leaving an opening for turning, sew pieces together; clip corners, turn right side out and press.

5. Stuff pillow with fiberfill; sew opening closed.

Banded Pillow

1. Cut two 17" squares from fabric for pillow front and back, a 10" x 33" piece for pillow band, and two 3¹/₂" x 33" pieces for band borders.

2. Matching right sides and raw edges and leaving an opening for turning, sew pillow front and back together. Clip corners, turn right side out, and press. Stuff pillow with fiberfill; sew opening closed.

3. Follow manufacturer's instructions to transfer image to center front of pillow band fabric piece.

4. Matching wrong sides, press each border fabric piece in half lengthwise. Matching long raw edges, stitch one border piece to wrong side of each long edge of band. Fold borders to front of band. Following manufacturer's instructions, use tape to fuse borders to front of band. Sew short ends together to complete pillow band; place band on pillow.

Layered Pillow

1. Cut two 17" squares from fabrics for pillow front and back, a 13" square for background, and a 10" square for transfer. Cut 9" squares and 11³/₄" squares from web.

2. Press raw edges of 13" fabric square ¹/₂" to wrong side; use 11³/₄" web square to fuse to center of pillow front fabric piece.

3. Follow manufacturer's instructions to transfer image to center of 10" fabric square; center and fuse 9" web square to wrong side. Remove threads to fringe edges of square; remove paper backing. Center and fuse fringed square to center of background square on pillow front.

4. Matching right sides and raw edges and leaving an opening for turning, sew pillow front and back together. Clip corners, turn right side out, and press. Stuff pillow with fiberfill; sew opening closed.

BIRDBATH WITH DRIED ARRANGEMENT

You will need a birdbath with base, cream and rust acrylic paint, paintbrushes, plastic foam ring to fit in birdbath, sheet moss, floral pins, decorative container to fit in center of foam ring, floral foam, and dried florals (we used bear grass, millet, ammobium, nigella, and white sierra bud).

Refer to Painting Basics, page 127, before beginning project. Allow paint to dry after each application.

1. Paint birdbath and base cream; *Dry Brush* with rust paint.

2. Cover foam ring with moss; secure with floral pins. Center ring in birdbath. Fill container with floral foam; place in center of ring.

3. Arrange bear grass around rim of container. Working toward center, add millet, then ammobium, nigella, and sierra bud.

TWIG BASKET

You will need pruning shears, straight twigs, household cement, 16" dia. grapevine wreath, and raffia.

1. Use pruning shears to cut twenty-four 16" and fourteen 10" twigs.

2. For bottom of basket, arrange and cement two 10" twigs across ends of ten evenly spaced 16" twigs.

3. Alternating 16" twigs for sides and 10" twigs for ends, cement remaining twigs together to form basket.

4. For handles, cut two 18¹/₂" lengths from grapevine wreath. Use cement and lengths of raffia to bind ends of each handle to basket corners.

PAINTED ROCKING CHAIR

You will need a wooden rocking chair with splat back; primer; ivory, light green, dark green, terra cotta, and brown acrylic paint; paintbrushes; 2"w foam brush; and wood-tone spray.

Refer to Painting Basics, page 127, before beginning project. Allow primer and paint to dry after each application.

1. Paint rocking chair with primer, then ivory paint.

2. Trace flowerpot pattern, page 117, onto tracing paper. Use transfer paper to transfer design onto splat. Paint flowerpot and topiary trunk using terra cotta, brown, and ivory paint. Using dark green, light green, then ivory paint, *Sponge Paint* topiary foliage.

3. Use dark green and terra cotta paint to add bands of color to chair turnings as desired.

4. Thin dark green paint with an equal amount of water. Use foam brush to paint vertical and horizontal stripes on chair seat to form a plaid design.

5. Thin terra cotta paint with an equal amount of water; use paint mixture to paint other areas on chair as desired.

6. Lightly spray chair with wood-tone spray.

WHEAT IN A TWIG VASE

You will need a 10" length of heavy cardboard tube, wood-tone spray, pruning shears, straight twigs, rubber bands, raffia, and dried wheat.

1. Spray tube with wood-tone spray; allow to dry.

2. Use pruning shears to cut 12" lengths of twigs; place around tube, holding in place with rubber bands. Knot several lengths of raffia around twigs, covering rubber bands.

3. Gather wheat into a bundle; trim stem ends and place in vase.

WHEAT TOPIARY IN CLAY POT

You will need dried wheat, rubber band, 4" dia. terra cotta flowerpot, floral foam, craft glue, sheet moss, and an 18" length of 2"w wired ribbon.

1. Gather wheat into a bundle and wrap with rubber band; trim stem ends.

2. Cut floral foam to fit in flowerpot; glue in place. Cut a 2" deep hole in foam wide enough to fit gathered wheat stems; place stems in hole and glue to secure. Cover foam surface with sheet moss; glue in place.

3. Wrap ribbon around wheat, covering rubber band; knot ribbon and trim ends.

WHEAT MOUND

You will need 4" dia. foam ball, 4" dia. terra cotta flowerpot, sheet moss, craft glue, floral or utility scissors, and dried wheat.

1. Push ball into flowerpot. Cover ball surface with sheet moss and glue in place.

2. Leaving $1/2$" of stem, cut wheat heads from stems. Placing wheat heads as close together as possible, insert stems into ball.

3. Trim wheat beards to form mound shape.

WOODSY LAMP AND SHADE

You will need an oval wooden plaque (ours measures $6^{1}/_2$" x 11"), eight $1/2$" dia. wooden cap buttons, hot glue gun, lamp kit with 11" bent (figurine-style) lamp pipe, brown floral tape, drill and bits, assorted small branches and twigs, preserved mosses (we used green mood and reindeer) and ferns, artificial birds' nest and eggs, self-adhesive lampshade, fabric, and $1/2$"w single-fold bias tape.

1. Glue wooden buttons to bottom of plaque for feet. Positioning off center, drill hole in plaque to fit lamp pipe. Wrap pipe with floral tape. Follow manufacturer's instructions to assemble lamp kit using plaque as base.

2. Beginning against pipe and building outward, glue branches and twigs to plaque to form desired arrangement. Arrange mosses, ferns, nest, and eggs around branches and glue in place.

3. Follow manufacturer's instructions to cover lampshade with fabric. Overlapping ends at fabric seam, glue bias tape around shade $1/4$" from top edge and $5/8$" from bottom edge. Place shade on lamp.

DECORATED FRAMES

You will need wooden picture frames, ivory spray paint, hot glue gun, and dried florals (we used sisal leaves, twigs, ammobium flowers, and raffia).

1. Paint frames.

2. Use hot glue to attach small bunches of flowers, leaves, or twigs (tied with raffia) to cover each frame as desired.

MOSAIC TOPPED TEA CART

You will need a teacart (we found ours at a flea market), piece of ¼" thick plywood to fit teacart top, newsprint, mastic (tile adhesive), trowel, assorted pieces of tiles and broken dishes, grout, and a sponge.

1. Cut a piece of newsprint same size as plywood. Arrange pieces of tile and dishes on newsprint as desired.

2. Follow manufacturer's instructions to apply mastic to plywood; transfer tile and dish pieces to prepared surface. Allow to dry.

3. Follow manufacturer's instructions to apply grout to tiled surface.

4. Place plywood on teacart.

BOTANICALS ON SLATE

For each project, you will need an 8" x 10" piece of slate with hanging holes; ivory and brown acrylic paint; foam brushes; botanical print with ivory background; spray adhesive; and 20" of 1½"w wired ribbon.

1. Paint front of slate ivory; allow to dry.

2. Apply spray adhesive to back of print. Position print at center of slate; smooth in place.

3. For wash, mix 1 part brown paint with 2 parts water. Paint front of slate with wash; wipe off excess.

4. For hanger, thread ends of ribbon through holes to front of slate. Tie a large knot in each end of ribbon so knots will not slip through holes.

SQUARE WREATH

You will need a corrugated cardboard box lid with 2" sides (ours measures 20" x 21"), craft knife, hot glue gun, and dried sisal leaves.

1. Cut an 8" x 9" opening in center of box lid.

2. Overlapping to cover entire cardboard surface, glue leaves on box lid.

LAYERED TOPIARY

You will need a 6" dia. terra cotta flowerpot, hot glue gun, floral foam, sheet moss, dried larkspur, sierra bud, ammobium, and nigella, and floral wire.

1. Trim larkspur stems to 17" long; trim sierra bud stems to 9" to 12" long. Place several stems of larkspur together. Arrange sierra around larkspur; wrap tightly with floral wire.

2. Place wired bundle in pot; use pieces of foam to tightly fill pot around bundle. Cover foam surface with moss.

3. Remove stems from nigella and ammobium. Glue two rows of nigella flower heads over wire. Glue clusters of ammobium around rim of flowerpot.

FLORAL CLOCK

You will need a clock in a ready-to-finish wooden frame with base, white primer, crackle medium, ivory and green acrylic paint, satin finish varnish, hot glue gun, dried ammobium and sierra bud flowers, and dried fern fronds.

1. Remove clock from frame; apply primer to frame and base.

2. Using green for basecoat and ivory for top coat, follow manufacturer's instructions to apply crackle finish to base only. Apply varnish; allow to dry.

3. Glue small bunches dried flowers in place to cover surface of clock frame. Trim with fern fronds and additional dried flowers.

4. Replace clock in frame.

GARDEN POTS WITH PAINTED ROSES

For each pot, you will need matte acrylic spray sealer; terra cotta flowerpots; white, green, pink, and red acrylic paint; and paintbrushes.

Refer to Painting Basics, page 127. Allow sealer and paint to dry after each application.

1. Spray pot with sealer.

2. *Dry Brush* an oval of white paint on each pot.

3. Follow *Painting Roses and Rosebuds*, page 41, to paint roses on white area.

RAKE PHOTO KEEPER

You will need a 4" dia. terra cotta pot, hand rake with flat tines, floral foam, excelsior, raffia, mini spring-type wooden clothespins, and acrylic paint to match rake handle.

1. Place rake handle in pot; use pieces of foam to tightly fill pot around handle. Cover foam surface with excelsior.

2. Tie raffia into a bow around rake.

3. Paint clothespins; allow to dry. Use clothespins to attach photos to rake tines.

BOTANICAL BUNDLES ON SHEER PANEL

You will need a sheer curtain panel, preserved florals (we used twigs, fern fronds, bear grass, and ammobium florets), needle, and heavy-duty thread.

1. Cut small pieces of preserved florals and gather into bundles; tie with thread.

2. Arrange bundles in rows on curtain panel. Working from the wrong side, stitch bundles in place.

PAINTING ROSES AND ROSEBUDS

DOUBLE LOAD:
Dip brush into water; blot on paper towel. Dip corner of brush into paint; dip the opposite corner of brush into

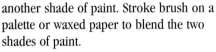

another shade of paint. Stroke brush on a palette or waxed paper to blend the two shades of paint.

HIGHLIGHT: Select a paint that is lighter than the area you want to highlight. Dip flat brush into water; blot on paper towel. Dip corner

of brush into paint; stroke brush on palette or waxed paper to blend. Stroke brush on area you wish to highlight.

"C" STROKE: Dip flat brush into water; blot on paper towel. Dip brush into paint; stroke brush on palette or waxed paper. Touch

brush to painting surface. Pull brush to the left and then downward in a curve. As you are pulling downward, apply pressure to create width of the "C". To end stroke, gradually release pressure on brush while pulling brush to the right.

COMMA STROKE:
Dip round brush into water; blot on paper towel. Dip brush into paint; touch brush tip to painting surface.

Apply slight pressure to brush to spread out brush hairs. Pull brush to the right or left in a curve. Gradually release pressure on brush to make tail of stroke.

LINE WORK: Mix paint with water to an ink-like consistency. Dip liner brush into thinned paint. Touch tip of brush to painting surface.

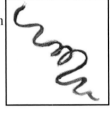

ROSEBUD

Paint colors: red, pink, white, and green.

Double load
brush in red and pink. With pink on top, make a "C"

stroke for top of bud, then make a "C" stroke for bottom of bud.

Use white to make **comma** strokes on top edges of bud. Use pink to make right and left **comma** strokes on either side of bud. Use green and **line work** for leaves and stem.

ROSE
Paint colors: red, pink, and white.

Double load
brush in red and pink. With pink on top, make a tight "C" stroke, wiggling

brush ot make ruffled edge of rose petal.

Make a circle of petals. Repeat for inner circle of rose.

Paint a rosebud in center of inner circle. **Highlight** edges of some petals using white.

sunny breakfast room

START THE DAY
WITH A CHEERY VIEW

Let the sun shine in this cheery breakfast room and get a bright start on the day! Bathed in heavenly hues — sunny yellows and sky blues — the room comes to life with furnishings brought in from the backyard and rejuvenated. Iron patio furniture, complemented by a host of naturally appealing accents, makes breakfast as refreshing as a walk in the park.

Ideal for use as a window treatment or cabinet enhancement, a rescued shutter carries the room's blue-and-white theme with a center stripe of matching mosaic and a collection of cups displayed with yellow gingham ribbons.

By simply adding table legs and decorative wood trim, a salvaged wooden toolbox (opposite) is rededicated to serve as an eye-catching flower box.

A scalloped seat cushion (opposite) softens the look and feel of an iron chair.

Reflecting simple charm, an old-fashioned juice pitcher (left) is a bright idea for a lamp.

A watering can (below) is given a new "old" finish that makes it appear as though you've just brought it in from the garden.

Trimmed with a frilly gingham bow, this handcrafted moss topiary is right at home in a clay flowerpot covered with a mosaic of broken blue-and-white china pieces.

Stretched art canvases (opposite, top) are embellished with half-round clay pots and bow-tied bouquets of faux jonquils and blue snowballs to add delightful dimension to the decor.

Revitalizing a plain patio tabletop into a mosaic masterpiece (opposite, bottom), broken blue dishes and pieces of yellow and blue glass form pretty flowers to become the focal point in this garden of sunshine.

sunny breakfast room

WATERING CAN

You will need a metal watering can, blue spray paint, paste floor wax, white gesso, and fine-grit sandpaper.

1. Spray paint can blue; allow to dry.

2. Apply a thin coat of wax to can.

3. Paint can with gesso; allow to dry.

4. Lightly sand can for a weathered look.

TOOLBOX PLANTER

You will need a wooden tool box with handle (we found ours at a flea market), four leg mounting brackets, four table legs, scalloped wooden molding, decorative wooden emblem, wood glue, 1" long finishing nails, fine-grit sandpaper, tack cloth, white and brown acrylic paint, paintbrushes, paste floor wax, and clear acrylic sealer.

Allow glue, paint, and sealer to dry after each application.

1. Following manufacturer's instructions, attach one mounting bracket to bottom of toolbox at each corner. Attach legs to mounting brackets.

2. Measure lower edge of each end of toolbox; cut pieces of molding to fit. Glue, then nail pieces in place on box. Measure across lower front of box, including ends of molding; cut molding to fit. Glue, then nail to box. Center wooden emblem on front of box and glue in place.

3. Sand planter and wipe with tack cloth; paint planter brown. Apply wax to planter. Paint planter white; sand lightly for a weathered look.

DIMENSIONAL ART ON CANVAS

For each project, you will need ivory and brown acrylic paint, paintbrushes, 9" x 12" artist's stretched canvas, fine-grit sandpaper, hot glue gun, 4"h half-round clay flowerpot, floral foam, small artificial flowers on stems (we used jonquils and blue snowballs), $1^1/_2$"w wired ribbon, and artificial sheet moss.

1. Allowing to dry between coats, paint canvas brown, then ivory. Lightly sand canvas for a weathered look.

2. Glue flowerpot to canvas. Fill flowerpot with foam. Gather flowers into a bundle; tie ribbon into a bow around flower stems. Insert stems into foam in flowerpot.

3. Cover foam surface with moss; glue to secure.

MOSAIC-TOPPED PATIO TABLE

You will need patio table (Our table top measures 36" in diameter; for a larger top, you will need additional plates and tiles.), safety goggles, heavy gloves, $1/_2$" plywood, saw, $3/_4$"w flexible wooden molding, small nails, white acrylic paint, paintbrush, six blue and white dinner plates, old bath towel, hammer, tile nippers, metal file, twelve 6" square white ceramic tiles, pieces of yellow glass, mastic (tile adhesive), putty knife, grout, tile float, and household sponge.

Wear safety goggles and heavy gloves when breaking plates and tiles.

1. Turn table upside down on plywood and draw around table top; cut out topper along drawn line. Place topper on table.

2. Aligning lower edges of molding and plywood so that top edge of molding forms a raised rim around plywood, nail molding in place.

3. Paint molding white; allow to dry.

4. Wrap each plate in towel and place on hard surface; use hammer to break into pieces. Arrange pieces around outer edge of table topper. Use nippers to shape some remaining plate pieces into petal shapes; file rough edges. Arrange petals into flower shapes.

5. For each flower center, break, shape, and file a piece of yellow glass; place at center of flower.

6. Refer to Step 4 to break tiles into pieces; use tile pieces and remaining plate pieces to fill in remaining surface of topper.

7. Lifting and replacing one piece at a time, use putty knife to apply a thick layer of tile adhesive to back of each piece of the mosaic design. Adjust pieces to form as level a surface as possible; allow to dry.

8. Use float and follow grout manufacturer's instructions to mix and apply grout.

MOSAIC WINDOW SHUTTERS

You will need two louvered wooden window shutters, white and brown acrylic paint, paintbrushes, fine-grit sandpaper, tack cloth, clear acrylic sealer, broken pieces of blue and white dishes, mastic (tile adhesive), putty knife, grout, tile float, household sponge, six 24" lengths of 1½"w wired ribbon, and six blue and white coffee cups.

Allow paint, sealer, adhesive, and grout to dry after each application.

1. Paint shutters white, then lightly dry brush with brown. Sand shutters for a weathered look and wipe with tack cloth; apply two coats of sealer.

2. Arrange pieces of broken dishes on center area of each shutter. Using a putty knife, apply a thick layer of tile adhesive to each piece and attach to shutter.

3. Use float and follow grout manufacturer's instructions to mix and apply grout over mosaic area.

4. Thread ribbons through louvers; tie into bows around handles of cups.

TOPIARY IN MOSAIC POT

You will need blue spray paint, 6" dia. clay flowerpot, paste floor wax, white gesso, paintbrushes, sandpaper, clear acrylic spray sealer, broken pieces of blue and white dishes and yellow glass, mastic (tile adhesive), grout, household sponge, duct tape, plaster of paris, large tin can, 20" length of 1" dia. stick, 6" dia. green plastic foam ball, craft glue, sheet moss, greening pins, white aquarium gravel, and a 30" length of 1½"w wired ribbon.

1. Spray paint rim of pot blue; allow to dry. Apply a thin layer of wax to rim. Apply gesso; allow to dry. Lightly sand rim; wipe with tack cloth. Apply sealer; allow to dry.

2. Using a putty knife, apply a thick layer of tile adhesive to back of each mosaic piece and attach pieces to cover remainder of pot.

3. Use float and follow grout manufacturer's instructions to mix and apply grout over dish pieces.

4. Use tape to seal hole in bottom of pot. Follow manufacturer's instructions to mix plaster in can; pour into pot. Place end of stick in plaster; allow to harden. Place gravel over surface of plaster.

5. Insert top of stick 4" into foam ball; remove. Apply craft glue to stick; replace ball.

6. Glue moss to surface of ball, using pins to hold moss in place. Allow glue to dry.

7. Tie ribbon into a bow around stick; notch streamers and shape as desired.

JUICE PITCHER LAMP

You will need a pitcher, small scrap of wood, saw, drill and bits, through-the-handle style lamp kit, sand or gravel, self-adhesive lampshade, fabric, hot glue gun, white piping, white bias tubing, and three white buttons.

1. Measure diameter of opening in top of pitcher. Cut circle from wood to fit into opening. Cut a hole in center of wooden circle to fit lamp pipe from kit. Follow kit manufacturer's instructions to assemble lamp on wooden circle.

2. Fill pitcher with sand or gravel. Glue wooden circle with lamp assembly into top of pitcher.

3. Follow manufacturer's instructions to cover lampshade with fabric. Glue piping along top and bottom edges of shade.

4. Folding ends to inside of shade, shape and glue bias tubing into a scallop design on front of lampshade. Glue buttons to lampshade.

SCALLOPED SEAT CUSHION

You will need chair with removable seat, 1" thick foam, fabric, white piping, and a staple gun.

1. Remove seat from chair. Draw around seat on foam and fabric. Cut out foam along drawn lines; cut out fabric 1" outside drawn line.

2. For each scallop on cushion cover, cut one 5" dia. circle from fabric. Fold each circle in half; cut on fold to make two half-circles. Matching raw edges, baste piping along curved edge on right side of one half-circle. Matching right sides, place half-circles together and stitch ¼" from curved edge; turn right side out and press. Repeat to make desired number of half circles for cushion.

3. Overlapping as necessary and matching raw edges, pin half circles along front and sides of seat fabric piece; baste in place.

4. Measure around outside of foam piece; add 2". Cut a 3"w strip from fabric the determined length. Press one long edge ¼" to wrong side; press ¼" to wrong side again and stitch in place. Matching right sides and raw edges, pin strip to seat fabric piece over half circles. Using a ½" seam allowance, sew pieces together.

5. Place foam on chair seat; place cushion cover over foam. Pulling taut, wrap cover to bottom of seat; staple to secure.

6. Reattach seat to chair.

zesty
dining
room

CITRUS THEME FILLS
ROOM WITH COLOR

Bring golden sunshine and natural freshness into your dining room with a delightful décor resplendent with clean, bright colors. From the nostalgic ladderback chairs and unique table to the hand-painted plates, wreath chandelier, and citrus-theme accents, this is a room to be enjoyed with food, family, and friends.

Classic ladderback chairs (opposite) with rush seats are finished with an aging glaze, then easily stenciled with décor-matching designs.

Our grapevine wreath chandelier (below) brings overhead beauty, displaying three pillar candles in terra-cotta saucers surrounded by silk lilacs, marigolds, and berries. Shirred fabric tubes conceal the wires from which the fixture is suspended.

Old-fashioned botanical citrus prints make a stunning impression when enlarged on a color photocopier and decoupaged on stretched artist's canvas. (The prints are reproduced on pages 120-122 for your convenience.)

Our handy sideboard server (opposite) matches the ladderback chairs both in finish and stenciled patterns. The simple porch-post candlesticks go beautifully with hand-painted birdhouses (shown close-up on page 60) and an arrangement of oranges – wonderfully fragrant additions to the natural ambience of the room.

A graceful garland (opposite) of grapevine, greenery, and cheerful flowers tops this window draped with sheer panels.

Stylish slipcovers for the upholstered chairs at each end of the table are sewn in pale plaid. Dainty frog closures and covered buttons hold them in place. Carpentry sawhorses support a table created with an interestingly painted wooden door. A glass top provides everyday protection.

Decoupage and hand-painting dress up our clear glass plates (opposite), set atop white metal chargers. Blossom-trimmed grapevine rings surround the handmade napkins. Charming painted flowerpots hold votives.

Papier-mache birdhouses (right) are given a weathered look.

Arranged in a terra-cotta saucer, the floral centerpiece (below) is a lively addition to the setting.

zesty dining room

DOOR DINING TABLE

You will need four 8' lengths of 2" x 4" lumber, saw, wooden door (our door measures 36" x 80"), drill with hole saw, wood glue, wood filler, two pairs of sawhorse brackets, sixteen 8-penny common nails, hammer, sandpaper, tack cloth, primer, yellow acrylic latex paint, paintbrushes, yellow ochre stencil paint (we used Delta™ Stencil Magic® Stencil Paint Creme), stencil brush, stick-on vinyl glass protector dots, and glass to fit door.

Allow, glue, wood filler, primer, paint, and sealer to dry after each application.

1. From lumber, cut eight pieces 27" long and two pieces 26" long.

2. Remove hardware from door. Use hole saw to cut a circle from scrap of 2" x 4" lumber to fit door knob hole. Glue circle in hole; allow to dry. Following manufacturer's instructions, use wood filler to fill smaller holes and cracks.

3. Follow bracket manufacturer's instructions to assemble sawhorses using 27" lumber pieces for legs and 26" pieces for top rails.

4. Sand door and lumber pieces; wipe with tack cloth. Apply primer, then two coats of latex paint to door, sawhorse brackets, and lumber pieces.

5. Use stencil paint and brush to dry brush highlights on door and legs.

6. Place door on sawhorses. Attach glass protector dots to glass; place glass on door.

SIDEBOARD SERVER

You will need a ready-to-finish side table; painter's masking tape; primer; paintbrushes; yellow and green acrylic paint; glazing medium (we used Ralph Lauren Aging and Technique Glaze®); waxed paper; vinyl stencil material; craft knife; cutting mat; white, yellow, green, and orange stencil paint (we used Delta™ Stencil Magic® Stencil Paint Creme); stencil brushes; and a gold paint pen.

Allow primer, paint, and glaze to dry after each application.

1. Sand table; wipe with tack cloth. Apply primer, then two coats of yellow paint to table. Use stencil paint and brush to dry brush yellow ochre highlights on table.

2. For border, measure and draw a line 2" from outside edge of table top; draw a second line ³/₄" inside first line. Place masking tape along both sides of border. Use stencil paint and brush to paint border orange; paint drawer pulls orange. Remove tape.

3. Place masking tape over orange border. Mix four parts glazing medium and one part green acrylic paint; use to paint inside masked area. While mixture is wet, blot with crumpled waxed paper. When dry, paint area again, using a mixture of one part glazing medium and one part yellow acrylic paint. While mixture is wet, blot with crumpled waxed paper. Remove masking tape.

4. Use patterns, page 65, and follow *Stenciling*, page 127, to stencil oranges, green leaves, and white buds on center of tabletop. Use liner brush to add yellow veins to leaves and orange highlights to buds. Use paint pen to outline stenciled designs.

LADDERBACK CHAIRS

You will need four ready-to-finish ladder-back chairs with rush seats; primer; paintbrushes; yellow and green acrylic paint; glazing medium (we used Ralph Lauren Aging and Technique Glaze®); vinyl stencil material; craft knife; cutting mat; white, yellow, green, and orange stencil paint (we used Delta™ Stencil Magic® Stencil Paint Creme); stencil brushes; and a gold paint pen.

1. Remove seats from chairs. Sand chairs; wipe with tack cloth. Apply primer, then two coats of yellow paint to chairs.

2. Mix one part green acrylic paint and four parts glazing medium. Lightly paint chair with glaze.

3. Use patterns, page 65, and follow *Stenciling*, page 127, to stencil oranges, green leaves, and white buds on chair back. Use liner brush to add yellow veins to leaves and orange highlights to buds. Use paint pen to outline stenciled designs and to add detail lines to turnings and slats of chair back. Use finger and stencil paint to add bands of color to turnings, if desired.

SLIPCOVER FOR UPHOLSTERED CHAIR

You will need newsprint, fabric, two pairs of large and two pairs of small frog closures, and a covered button kit with two ³/₄" buttons.

Our instructions will make one slipcover. Refer to Fig. 1 for all measuring. Use a ¹/₂" seam allowance unless otherwise indicated.

1. Measure across front of chair seat (A) and across back of chair seat (B); measure depth of chair seat (C). Use these measurements to draw pattern for chair seat on newsprint; draw a second line 1/2" outside the first. Cut out pattern on outside line. Use pattern to cut one piece from fabric.

Fig. 1

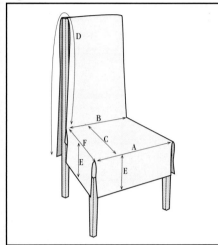

2. For chair back cover, measure from back of chair seat, over back of chair and down to bottom of desired skirt length (D); add 1". Measure across back of chair seat (B); add 1". Cut a piece of fabric the determined measurements.

3. For front skirt piece, measure desired length of the skirt and add 1". Measure across front of chair seat (A); add 1" Cut a piece of fabric the determined measurements.

4. For side skirt pieces, measure the desired length of the skirt and add 1". Measure along side of chair seat (F); add 1". Cut two pieces of fabric the determined measurements.

5. To make hems, press raw edges 1/4" to wrong side; press 1/4" to wrong side again and stitch in place. Hem both long edges and one short edge of chair back cover piece. Hem both short edges and one long edge of each skirt piece.

6. Matching right sides and raw edges; stitch chair back cover to back of chair seat cover; stitch front skirt piece to front of chair seat cover, and stitch side skirt pieces to sides of chair back cover. Press slipcover.

7. Follow manufacturer's instructions to cover two buttons with fabric.

8. Place slipcover on chair; determine positions for frog closures. Use fabric glue to attach large closures to chair back cover; glue loop ends of closures together and glue buttons over loops. Glue small closures to chair skirt.

GRAPEVINE WINDOW TOPPER
You will need small nails, crown grapevine swag, two corner grapevine swags, artificial greenery garland, floral wire, artificial greenery and flowers.

1. Use small nails to attach to grapevine pieces to wall around top of window.

2. Arrange garland over grapevine pieces, using small lengths of floral wire to secure as necessary.

3. Inserting stems into grapevine, arrange additional greenery, then flowers on crown swag.

GRAPEVINE WREATH CHANDELIER
You will need a drill and bits, three 4" dia. terra cotta plant saucers, white and green acrylic paint, paintbrushes, picture hanging wire, 17" dia. grapevine wreath, fabric, artificial flowers (we used four stems of lilacs and three stems each of marigolds and berries), hot glue gun, floral wire, and three pillar candles.

1. Drill two holes 2" apart in bottom of each saucer.

2. Dry brush saucers with white paint. Dry brush wreath with green paint.

3. Cut three two-yard lengths of picture wire. Spacing evenly, attach one end of each wire to wreath, threading wire through grapevine; wrap wire end around itself to secure.

4. Cut three 4" x 60" strips from fabric. Matching right sides and long edges, fold each strip in half; stitch 1/2" from long edges to form tube. Turn right side out. Folding raw ends to inside, place one tube over each wire. Bring free ends of wire together above center of wreath; beginning 24" above wreath, twist wires together. To make hanger, form twisted wire into a 6" loop, wrapping tail ends of wire around bottom of loop to secure.

5. Cutting into smaller sections as necessary, arrange flowers and berries on wreath and glue in place.

6. Referring to Fig. 1, use a 10" length of floral wire to attach saucers to wreath.

Fig. 1

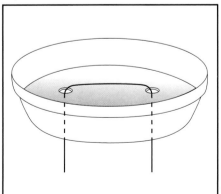

7. Suspend wreath from ceiling. (We used a screw-in hook.) Place candles in saucers.

FLORAL CENTERPIECE

You will need 8" dia. terra cotta plant saucer, white and green acrylic paint, paintbrush, sponge piece, floral foam, hot glue gun, sheet moss, greening pins, artificial flowers and greenery (we used three stems each of lilac, gerber daisies, alstromeria, freesia, and berries, curly willow and ivy), wire cutters.

Refer to Painting Basics, page 127, before beginning project.

1. *Dry Brush* saucer with white paint; *Sponge Paint* lightly with green.

2. Glue floral foam in saucer; cover with moss, using greening pins to secure.

3. Using wire cutters to trim stems as necessary and working from center of saucer outward, insert stems of larger flowers into foam. Fill in with smaller flowers and ivy.

CITRUS PRINTS ON CANVAS

For each print, you will need painter's masking tape; yellow and green acrylic paint; paintbrushes; 12" x 24" artist's stretched canvas; acrylic spray sealer; decoupage medium; glazing medium; foam brushes; broad-tipped gold paint pen; $2^1/_8$ yds. of $^3/_4$"w gimp trim; and a hot glue gun.

Allow sealer, paint, and decoupage medium to dry after each application.

1. Apply a length of tape 2" from each end of canvas; paint top and bottom 2" green. Remove tape. Draw a straight line with paint pen covering edge of painted area.

2. At copy shop, have color copy made of desired citrus print, pages 120 through 122, enlarging 157%.

3. Apply two coats of sealer to canvas and to each side of photocopy.

4. Apply a mixture of two parts decoupage medium and one part water to front of canvas and to back of photocopy. While wet, position photocopy on center of canvas; use foam brush to brush with thinned decoupage medium, smoothing out air bubbles as print dries. Apply two additional coats of decoupage medium.

5. Apply two coats of sealer to canvas.

6. Mix a small amount of yellow paint with glazing medium; apply to surface of canvas.

7. Hot glue gimp around outside of canvas, covering staples.

SALAD PLATES AND CHARGERS

You will need six 9" dia. clear glass salad plates, yellow and green glass paint (we used a Delta Air Dry PermEnamel™ glass paint starter kit), flat and liner paintbrushes, six white metal chargers (we used a combination of plain and scalloped chargers), small sharp scissors, clear acrylic spray sealer, and decoupage medium.

Carefully follow paint kit manufacturer's instructions to prepare surface and apply paint to plates.

1. Use flat and liner brushes and yellow and green paint to paint back of each plate flange with wide and narrow lines to form a plaid design.

2. At copy shop, have color copies made of citrus print, page 119. Use scissors to carefully cut desired motifs from photocopies.

3. Allowing to dry between coats, apply two coats of spray sealer to each side of each motif.

4. Follow manufacturer's instructions to decoupage one motif to center of each charger.

NAPKINS AND NAPKIN RINGS

You will need $1^3/_4$ yds. of 45"w fabric, six 3" dia. grapevine wreaths, six artificial marigolds, six pieces of artificial greenery, green covered floral wire, wire cutters, and a hot glue gun.

1. For napkins, cut six 20" squares from fabric. On each square, press two opposite edges $^1/_4$" to wrong side; press $^1/_4$" to wrong side again and stitch in place. Repeat with remaining raw edges.

2. For each napkin ring, curl a 10" length of wire around a pencil. Glue center of wire to one wreath. Glue one piece of greenery and one marigold over center of wire.

3. Fold each napkin and place in napkin ring.

BIRDHOUSES

You will need one large and one small papier-mâché birdhouse, glossy wood-tone spray; paste floor wax, fine grip sandpaper; cream, yellow, orange, and green acrylic paint; flat and liner paintbrushes, clear acrylic spray sealer, and Spanish moss.

Allow paint and sealer to dry after each application.

1. Spray birdhouses with wood-tone spray. Wax lightly; paint cream and allow to dry. Sand birdhouses lightly for a weathered look.

2. Thin yellow, orange, and green paints with small amounts of water. Paint roof of small birdhouse green; paint base of large birdhouse orange. Use flat and liner brushes and all three paint colors to paint roof of large birdhouse with wide and narrow lines to form a plaid design.

3. Spray each birdhouse with two coats of sealer.

4. Place a small amount of moss in each birdhouse opening.

PORCH POST CANDLESTICKS
You will need a saw, three wooden spindles, three 3" dia. terra cotta plant saucers, drill and bit, three 2" long wood screws, glossy wood-tone spray, paste floor wax, white acrylic paint, paintbrush, and fine-grit sandpaper.

1. Use saw to cut each spindle to desired height. Drill a hole in the center bottom of each saucer. Use screw to attach one saucer to top of each spindle.

2. Spray each candlestick with wood-tone paint; allow to dry. Wax lightly; paint white and allow to dry. Sand each candlestick lightly for a weathered look.

TERRA COTTA VOTIVES
For each votive holder, you will need a 2¹/₂" dia. terra cotta pot; white, yellow, and green acrylic paint; paintbrush; sponge piece, and a votive candle.

1. Dry brush flowerpot with white paint. Sponge paint pot lightly with yellow, then green paint.

2. Place candle in holder.

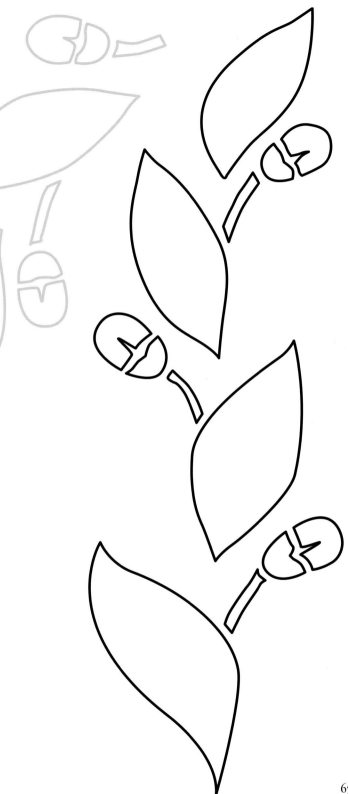

home office haven

OPENING THE DOOR TO SUCCESS

Introduce the peacefulness of a warm spring afternoon into your home office with this quiet and comfortable collection of transplanted outdoor furnishings and garden gadgets. You'll almost hear the dragonflies buzzing happily through the room while you work at your spacious desk, which is created from a timeworn door. With a cozy cushioned garden bench and a shuttered screen to block distractions, your office will be a haven where you can relax and get down to business!

Screening out household distractions will be a breeze when you utilize a pair of our two-shutter shelf units (opposite). Or add balance to the room by separating them. Either way, you can organize helpful reminders, family photos, and knickknacks on the handy painted shelves and racks to set a casual mood without infringing on your workspace.

Get in the frame of mind to work by opening this simple Roman window shade (below) trimmed with dragonfly fabric transfers to let the sun shine in on your desk. The spacious glass-topped table is crafted from a wooden door decorated with a distressed painting technique and preserved leaves. Dressed-up mats help the dragonfly prints coordinate.

Staying organized will be easier than ever with this functional fabric-covered filing cabinet (this page) and playful recycling bucket.

You'll be sitting pretty in our fashionable plaid slipcovered chair (opposite). A comfy pillow is embellished with the room's recurring dragonfly design, while the coordinating fabric border on the sisal rug easily makes the room appear more home than office.

You'll be refreshed each time you gaze at this refurbished watering can lamp (opposite) with decorated shade, as well as when you see our stylish painted flowerpot pencil holder and dragonfly terra-cotta vase.

The calming babble of this tabletop birdbath water fountain (this page) will soothe the stress of meeting office deadlines while adding a touch of whimsy to the décor. And the window frame organizer, with cork area and chalkboard, will make sure you stay too busy to daydream out the window.

A matched set of dragonfly etchings adds classic style to the room when arranged in rustic painted frames with fabric mats.

We used the pillows of this cozy garden bench to tie together several of the decorating motifs within the room. The result is an irresistible image of garden tranquillity!

home office haven

DOOR WRITING TABLE

You will need a wooden door (our door measures 30" x 78"); drill with hole saw; scrap of 2" x 4" lumber; wood filler; wood glue; three 8' lengths of 1" x 4" lumber; saw; 1", 1³/₄", and 4" long flathead wood screws; six 2" corner braces; four 28" long table legs; sandpaper; tack cloth; primer; ivory and gold acrylic latex paint; crackling medium; paintbrushes; preserved skeleton leaves; spray adhesive; waxed paper; stick-on vinyl glass protector dots; and glass to fit door.

Allow wood filler, primer, and paint to dry after each application.

1. Remove hardware from door. Use hole saw to cut a circle from scrap of 2" x 4" lumber to fit door knob hole. Glue circle in hole; allow to dry. Following manufacturer's instructions, use wood filler to fill smaller holes and cracks.

2. Measure height and width of door; cut two pieces of 1" x 4" lumber 8" shorter than each measurement. Referring to Fig. 1, use 1³/₄" screws to assemble pieces to form apron for writing table.

Fig. 1

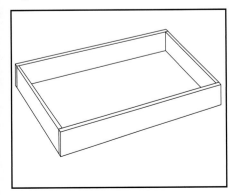

3. Centering apron on door and spacing braces evenly, use 1" long screws and corner braces to attach apron to door. Use 1³/₄" long screws to attach one table leg to each inside corner of apron. With table upright, drive one 4" long screw through door and into top of each table leg.

4. Sand writing table; wipe with tack cloth and apply primer. Paint door only with two coats of gold paint. Follow crackling medium instructions to apply crackle finish to door, using ivory for top coat. Paint apron and legs with two coats of ivory paint.

5. Spray wrong sides of leaves with spray adhesive. Use waxed paper to press leaves in place on tabletop.

6. Attach glass protector dots to glass; place glass on tabletop.

PINEAPPLE FINIAL FOUNTAIN

You will need concrete pineapple finial, drill with ¹/₄" and ¹/₂" dia. masonry bits, waterproof spray sealer, 10¹/₂" dia. pedestal bowl, 12" length of ³/₈" dia. wooden dowel, indoor/outdoor fountain pump, 9¹/₂" length of ¹/₂" dia. plastic tubing, artificial ivy garland, sheet moss, silicone sealer, and small smooth stones.

1. Drill a ¹/₂" dia. hole up through base of finial; drill a ¹/₄" hole down through top of finial. Apply sealer to outside of finial, inside of drilled holes, and inside and outside of bowl.

2. Slip dowel into tubing. Apply a generous amount of silicone sealer to one end of tubing; use dowel to slide end of tubing with silicone sealer through hole in base of finial up to hole in top of finial.

Press tubing and silicone sealer against finial at hole to secure. Allow silicone sealer to set; remove dowel.

3. Attach tubing to pump. Place pump and finial inside bowl.

4. Arrange stones around finial. Use silicone sealer to secure ivy and moss to fountain.

WINDOW MESSAGE BOARD

You will need a wood-framed window with three panes (we found ours at a flea market), sandpaper, tack cloth, ivory and gold acrylic paint, crackling medium, paintbrushes, hardboard, saw, sheet cork, spray adhesive, fabric, hot glue gun, chalkboard paint, and glazier's points.

1. Remove and discard glass from window. Scrape away any caulk or sealer; sand window frame and wipe with tack cloth.

2. Using gold paint for base coat and cream for top coat, follow crackle medium manufacturer's instructions to paint window.

3. For each pane, measure opening; cut a piece of hardboard ¹/₄" larger on all sides than opening.

4. For message board, cut a sheet of cork the same size as one hardboard piece. Use spray adhesive to attach cork to smooth side of hardboard.

5. Cut fabric 1" larger on all sides than one hardboard piece. Center hardboard on wrong side of fabric; pulling fabric taut and folding at corners, wrap fabric edges to wrong side and use hot glue to secure.

6. At copy shop, have desired print, pages 123 through 126, color copied onto card stock. Trim copy to appropriate size; use spray adhesive to attach to center of fabric-covered board.

7. Follow manufacturer's instructions to apply chalkboard paint to smooth side of remaining piece of hardboard.

8. Use glazier's points to mount each hardboard piece in one window opening.

LOUVERED DOOR SHELF UNITS

For each set of shelves, you will need a hinged pair of louvered doors, $1/4$" plywood, 1"w molding, wood glue, small finishing nails, $1/2$" x $3/4$" plain molding, 1" long wood screws, 2" corner braces, ivory and gold acrylic paint, paintbrushes, and crackle medium.

1. For shelves, measure width of one door. Use measurement to cut a square of plywood; cut square in half diagonally to make two shelves. Repeat to make desired number of shelves.

2. Cut a length of molding 1" longer than the front (long) edge of each triangular shelf. Centering molding on shelf front, use glue then small nails to secure. To miter ends of molding, trim at a 45-degree angle.

3. For braces for each shelf, cut two lengths of $1/2$" x $3/4$" molding $1/2$" shorter than door width determined in Step 1. Miter ends of each length by trimming at a 45-degree angle.

4. Determine and mark locations for shelves. With long edge of each brace against door, glue and then nail one brace to front of each door.

5. Fold doors at right angles and use screws to attach a corner brace to back of doors at each hinge.

6. Paint outside frame only of each door with two coats of gold paint. Follow crackle medium instructions to apply crackle finish to door frame, using ivory for top coat. Paint remainder of doors and shelves with two coats of ivory paint. Allow to dry completely.

7. Place shelves on brackets.

SLIP-COVERED CHAIR

You will need newsprint, fabric, covered button kit with four $1^1/2$" buttons, and self-adhesive hook and loop fastener dots.

1. For patterns, draw around chair back and chair seat on newsprint. Measure thickness of chair back; divide by 2 and add $1/2$". Using the determined measurement, draw a second line outside the first on chair back pattern. Draw a second line $1/2$" outside first line on seat pattern. Cut out patterns on outside lines.

2. Using patterns, cut two chair back pieces and one seat piece from fabric.

3. Place chair back pieces right sides together. If chair back is wider at top than at bottom, place a mark on each side of fabric pieces at widest point; if chair back is same width from top to bottom, place marks 14" from bottom edge of fabric pieces.

4. Using a $1/2$" seam allowance, sew chair back pieces together across top between marks. Below mark on each side of chair back cover, hem each raw edge by pressing $1/4$" to wrong side, pressing $1/4$" to wrong side again, and stitching in place.

5. For skirt front, measure inside line on front and sides only of chair seat pattern, multiply by 3 and add 1". Measure distance from top edge of chair seat to

floor; add 3". Piecing as necessary, cut a piece of fabric the determined measurements.

6. Press each short edge of skirt $1/4$" to wrong side; press $1/4$" to wrong side again and stitch. For bottom hem, press one long edge of skirt $1/2$" to wrong side; press 2" to wrong side and stitch in place.

7. Place chair seat fabric piece right side up on flat surface. Matching right sides and raw edges, pin center front of skirt to center front of seat fabric; pin each end of skirt fabric piece $1/2$" from back edge of seat piece.

8. Fold fabric to form three evenly-spaced box pleats along front of seat fabric piece; pin in place. Repeat to form three box pleats on each side of seat piece. Using a $1/2$" seam allowance, sew pleated skirt to front and sides of seat fabric piece.

9. Matching right sides, stitch remaining raw edge (back) of chair seat fabric piece to lower front raw edge of chair back cover.

10. For skirt back, measure lower back raw edge of chair back cover; multiply by 3 and add 1". Using this number and the seat-to-floor measurement determined in Step 3, cut fabric piece for skirt back. Repeat Step 6 to hem skirt back.

11. Fold raw edge of skirt back to form three evenly-spaced box pleats; pin in place. Matching right sides, stitch raw pleated edge of skirt back to lower raw edge of chair back cover.

12. Follow manufacturer's instructions to cover buttons with fabric. On each side of slipcover, sew one button to top of opening and one button 1" above skirt seam on front of opening.

13. Attach hook half of one hook and loop fastener to wrong side of slipcover opening under each lower button. Place slipcover on chair and adjust to fit. Overlapping front and back of each side opening, mark position and attach corresponding loop half of fastener to back of opening.

BORDERED SISAL RUG

You will need a 60" x 96" sisal rug; two 12" x 60" and two 12" x 96" strips of fabric, and a hot glue gun.

1. Press one long raw edge of each fabric strip 2" to wrong side. Press opposite edge 4" to wrong side. Press ends of short fabric strips to center fold to form miter (Fig. 1).

Fig. 1

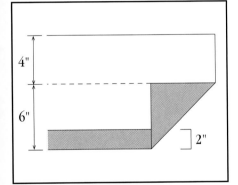

2. Inserting edges of rug into folds of each strip, glue long, then short strips to corresponding edges of rug.

FRAMED DRAGONFLY PRINTS

You will need four 11" x 14" wooden picture frames, ivory and metallic gold acrylic paint, crackle medium, paintbrushes, four 11" x 14" mats with 5" x 7" openings, fabric, spray adhesive, acid-free paper tape, four 11" x 14" pieces of cardboard, glazier's points, four picture hangers.

1. Using gold paint for base coat and cream for top coat, follow crackle

medium manufacturer's instructions to paint each frame.

2. To cover each mat, cut fabric 2" larger on all sides than mat. Spray front of mat with spray adhesive; center on wrong side of fabric. Cutting to within 1/8" of inside corners, cut an X in mat opening. Pulling fabric taut and folding at corners, wrap fabric edges to wrong side; use hot glue to secure.

3. At copy shop, have prints, pages 123 through 126, color copied onto card stock. On wrong side of fabric-covered mat, center print over opening and tape in place.

4. Place each matted print, then cardboard in frame. Use glazier's points to secure. Attach hanger to frame.

DRAGONFLY DESK ACCESSORIES

You will need assorted containers (we used a galvanized metal pail, rectangular box with handles, and vase and terra cotta flowerpots and saucers), primer; ivory, green, dark green, and metallic gold acrylic paint; paintbrushes; color photocopies of desired dragonfly prints, pages 123 through 126; small, sharp scissors; acrylic spray sealer; decoupage medium; foam brushes; black fine-point permanent marker, cardboard; fabric; and a hot glue gun.

1. Apply primer and two coats of ivory paint to each container.

2. Use small sharp scissors to cut dragonflies from prints. Apply two coats of sealer to each side of dragonfly cutouts.

3. Follow manufacturer's instructions to decoupage dragonflies on containers.

4. Use marker to draw antennae and legs on dragonflies and to add sayings to

containers, if desired (ours say "dreaming away lazy days in the garden").

5. For painted details on containers, add bands of gold paint or use flat and liner brushes and green, dark green, and gold paint to paint wide and narrow lines to form a plaid design.

6. To line box with fabric, measure inside of box, adding 1/4" to height of side and end; cut out paper templates for side, end, and bottom of box. Using templates, cut one bottom, two end, and two side pieces from cardboard. From fabric, cut pieces 1" larger on all sides than cardboard pieces. Center each cardboard piece on wrong side of corresponding fabric piece; pulling fabric taut and folding at corners, wrap fabric edges to wrong side and use hot glue to secure. Glue covered cardboard pieces to inside surfaces of box.

DRAGONFLY SCRAPBOOK

You will need a scrapbook (ours measures 11" x 12"), 7" square of plaid fabric, 6" square of paper-backed fusible web, medium-point black permanent marker, acrylic spray sealer, and a hot glue gun.

1. Center and fuse web square to wrong side of fabric square. Remove threads to fringe fabric edges. Remove paper backing and fuse fabric square to center front of scrapbook cover.

2. At copy shop, have desired dragonfly print, pages 123 through 126, copied onto parchment card stock. Trim card to measure 4 1/2" square. Use marker to add wording, if desired.

3. Allowing to dry after each coat, spray each side of card with two coats of sealer. Center card on fabric square and hot glue in place.

FABRIC-TRIMMED FILE CABINET

You will need a two-drawer wooden filing cabinet, sandpaper, tack cloth, primer, ivory paint, paintbrushes, poster board, fusible fleece, fabric, hot glue gun, and an awl.

1. Sand filing cabinet surfaces that are to be painted; wipe with tack cloth. Allowing to dry after each application, apply primer then two coats of ivory paint.

2. For each surface of file cabinet to be covered with fabric, measure area and cut a piece of poster board $1/8$" smaller on all sides. Cut one piece of fleece the same size and one piece of fabric 1" larger on all sides than poster board.

3. Follow manufacturer's instructions to fuse fleece to poster board. Center poster board fleece side down on wrong side of fabric piece. Folding at corners and pulling fabric taut, hot glue edges of fabric to back of poster board. Hot glue fabric-covered panel in place on cabinet. (Note: For drawer front panels, remove drawer pulls and mark location for screws on poster board; use awl to punch holes in covered panels before attaching panel to drawer front.)

WATERING CAN LAMP

You will need a metal watering can; primer; ivory, green, dark green, and metallic gold acrylic paint; regular, flat, and liner paintbrushes; lamp kit with straight pipe 6" longer than height of watering can; sand or aquarium gravel; self-adhesive lampshade, fabric, and artificial greenery bush.

1. Allowing to dry after each application, apply primer and two coats of ivory paint to watering can.

2. Referring to photo, use flat and liner brushes and green, dark green, and gold

paint to paint front of watering can with wide and narrow lines to form a plaid design.

3. Drill hole in bottom of can to fit pipe from lamp kit. Follow manufacturer's instructions to assemble lamp kit in watering can.

4. Fill can with sand or gravel. Push stem of greenery bush into sand or gravel; arrange vines over can opening.

5. Follow manufacturer's instructions to cover lampshade with fabric. Place shade on lamp.

GARDEN BENCH CUSHION

You will need 2" thick foam, fabric, and matching thread.

1. Measure width and length of seat, cut foam to fit. Cut two pieces of fabric 2" larger on each side than foam.

2. Matching right sides and raw edges and leaving a long opening to insert foam, use a $1/2$" seam allowance to sew fabric pieces together.

3. Referring to Fig. 1, press each corner flat, matching seams. Stitch across point to form box corner; trim $1/4$" from stitching line.

Fig. 1

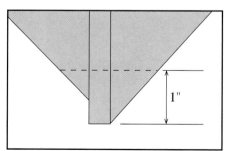

4. Turn cover right side out; insert foam and sew opening closed.

LARGE PILLOW

For each pillow, you will need $5/8$ yd. of green plaid fabric, matching thread, and a 20" square pillow form.

1. Cut two 21" squares from fabric.

2. Matching right sides and raw edges and leaving an opening for turning, use a $1/2$" seam allowance to sew fabric pieces together. Clip corners, turn right side out, and press. Insert pillow form; sew opening closed.

DRAGONFLY BORDER PILLOW

For each pillow, you will need muslin and green plaid fabrics, paper-backed fusible web, matching thread, green embroidery floss, 16" square pillow form, hot glue gun, and a small metal dragonfly cutout.

1. Cut 17" squares from muslin and plaid fabric; cut an 8" square from plaid fabric and a 7" square from web.

2. Center and fuse web square to wrong side of 8" plaid square; remove threads to fringe edge of plaid square. Remove paper backing and fuse square to center of muslin square for pillow front. Use six strands of floss to work a cross-stitch in each corner of plaid square.

3. At copy shop, have color copies of desired dragonfly prints, pages 123 through 126, made on photo transfer paper. Follow paper manufacturer's instructions to transfer images to muslin area of pillow front.

4. Matching right sides and raw edges and leaving an opening for turning, stitch pillow front and 17" plaid square together. Clip corners, turn right side out and press. Insert pillow form; sew opening closed.

5. Use household cement to attach dragonfly cutout to pillow front; allow to dry.

SMALL DRAGONFLY PILLOW

You will need green plaid fabric, muslin, matching thread, paper-backed fusible web, green embroidery floss, and a 14" square pillow form.

1. Cut two 15" squares from plaid fabric, a 7" square from muslin, and a 6½" square from web.

2. Center and fuse web square to wrong side of muslin square. Remove threads to fringe edges of muslin square; fuse to center of one plaid square.

3. At copy shop, have color copy of desired dragonfly print, pages 123 through 126, made on photo transfer paper. Follow paper manufacturer's instructions to transfer image to center of muslin square.

4. Use six strands of floss to work a cross-stitch at each corner of muslin square.

5. Matching right sides and raw edges and leaving an opening for turning, use a ½" seam allowance to stitch plaid squares together. Clip corners, turn right side out and press. Insert pillow form; sew opening closed.

ROMAN WINDOW SHADE

You will need fabrics for shade and lining, muslin, paper-backed fusible web, ring tape (available at drapery supply stores), staple gun, 1" x 2" lumber, metal screw eyes, fine polyester drapery cord, 2" long drywall screws, and a cord cleat.

1. Measuring inside window molding, measure width of window and add 1"; measure length of window and add 5".

Use the determined measurements to cut pieces from shade and lining fabrics.

2. Cut a strip of muslin 5½" by the width determined in Step 1; cut fusible web 5"w by determined width. Center web on muslin strip and fuse in place; do not remove paper backing. Remove threads to fringe long edges of strip.

3. At copy shop, have color copies of desired dragonfly prints, pages 123 through 126, made on photo transfer paper. Follow paper manufacturer's instructions to transfer images to center of muslin strip. Remove paper and fuse muslin 6" from bottom of shade fabric piece.

4. To determine number of ring tapes needed, divide width of lining by ten and round up to nearest whole number. Cutting through tape ½" below a ring and cutting lengths of tape 10" shorter than length of lining, cut determined number of tapes. Referring to Fig. 1 and keeping rings aligned, arrange tapes on lining and topstitch in place.

Fig. 1

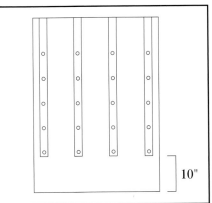

5. Matching right sides and raw edges and leaving an opening for turning, use a ½" seam allowance to sew shade and lining pieces together. Clip corners, turn right side out, press, and sew opening

closed. With matching thread, stitch over each ring, catching lining and shade fabric.

6. Press bottom of shade 2" to wrong side; topstitch in place.

7. For mounting board, cut 1" x 2" lumber ¼" shorter than width of shade. Wrapping and stapling in place, cover board with shade fabric. Staple top of shade to mounting board.

8. Attach a screw eye to underside of mounting board at the top of each row of ring tape.

9. Place shade lining side up on a flat surface. Referring to Fig. 2, tie a length of cord to bottom ring of one tape; thread cord up through all rings on that tape and through screw eyes to side of shade. Repeat for each remaining tape. Knot cords together at side of shade and again near bottom of shade; trim cord ends.

Fig. 2

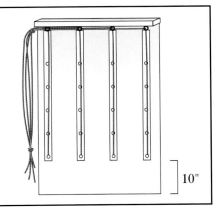

10. Using screws, mount board to inside top of window frame and cord cleat to side of window next to cords. Pull cords to lift shade to desired level; wrap cords around cleat.

refreshing bedroom

LAVENDER BRINGS FRAGRANT LUXURY

Cool, crisp colors and herb-garden freshness create a dreamy illusion in this beautiful bedroom. Our simple, romantic setting is highlighted by fragrant bundles of lavender, soft candlelight, and luxurious textures. A restful sleep is insured amidst the fresh white décor and serene softness of plump, inviting pillows. Easy crafting, sewing, and painting techniques make it a breeze to transform this delightful room.

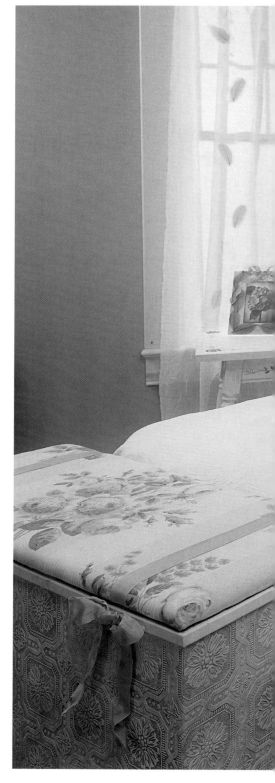

Preserved leaves float in barely-there pockets on our sheer curtain panels. The charming bedside table, shown in its entirety on page 88, is easily transformed from unfinished furniture with white paint and a green color wash. Traditional floral patterns highlight the simple table.

Additional preserved leaves look fresh and natural atop a sheer pillow sham (opposite). A no-sew floral-print bolster pillow echoes the soft hues of the color-washed headboard with hand-painted flowers.

A weathered clay pot (opposite) makes an elegant base for a dramatic lavender topiary. The beribboned arrangement is assembled using a cardboard tube covered with preserved leaves.

Skeleton leaves are again used to embellish a picture frame (below) and hurricane globe. The leafy frame exhibits a colorful botanical print mounted on handmade paper. Our leaf-graced globe is easily adorned and placed on a lacy paper doily.

Complement storage space with an old-fashioned hope chest, covered with embossed wallpaper resembling antique tin ceiling tiles. Dainty feet made of fence-post caps enhance the chic style. Add softness with a floral padded lid on the chest and on a coordinating picnic basket, shown on page 81, for holding guest-room luxuries.

For a compelling conversation piece, create a moss-covered console
shelf (above, left) to display knickknacks; finish with a freeze-dried gardenia.

Squares of embossed wallpaper are color-washed and folded into cone-shaped
sconces to hold nosegays of lavender.

Easy-to-paint floral patterns add charm to this color-washed table.

refreshing bedroom

SHEER PILLOW SHAM

You will need a purchased pillow, sheer fabric, three preserved skeleton leaves, tulle, and embroidery floss.

Use a $1/2$" seam allowance for all sewing unless otherwise indicated.

1. Measure height and width of pillow; add 1" to each measurement; multiply height by two. Use the determined measurements to cut a piece from sheer fabric.

2. Press short edges of fabric piece $1/4$" to wrong side; press $1/4$" to wrong side again and stitch in place.

3. Matching right sides and hemmed edges, fold fabric piece in half. Sew raw edges at each end together; turn right side out.

4. Cut six 2" x 13" strips from sheer fabric. For each tie, match right sides and long edges to fold each strip in half. Using a $1/4$" seam allowance, sew long edges together to form a tube. Turn tie right side out; tuck raw ends to inside and stitch in place. Spacing evenly, stitch pairs of ties to open edges of sham.

5. For pocket, cut a 5" x 8" piece of tulle. Centering pocket on front of sham, use three strands of embroidery floss to work *Running Stitch*, page 127, along sides and bottom of pocket. Spacing evenly, stitch two vertical lines to divide pocket into thirds.

6. Place a leaf in each pocket; working from inside sham, tack leaves in place. Place pillow in sham; knot ties to close.

SHEER WINDOW TREATMENT

You will need tulle, purchased sheer curtain panel, embroidery floss, and preserved skeleton leaves.

1. For each pocket, cut a $4^{1}/_{2}$" square from tulle.

2. Arrange pockets on panel as desired. Using three strands of embroidery floss, work *Running Stitch*, page 127, to sew sides and bottom of each pocket in place.

3. Place a leaf in each pocket. Working from wrong side, tack each leaf in place.

BOTANICAL PRINT IN LEAFY FRAME

You will need a 4" x 6" botanical print, 8" x 10" piece of handmade paper, spray adhesive, 8" x 10" acrylic picture frame, preserved skeleton leaves, waxed paper, $^{7}/_{8}$"w wired ribbon and a hot glue gun.

1. Use spray adhesive to mount print in center of handmade paper. Place mounted print in frame.

2. Spray wrong sides of leaves with spray adhesive. Use waxed paper to press leaves in place along outer edge of frame; allow to dry.

3. Tie ribbon into a bow; trim and notch streamer ends. Use hot glue to attach bow to frame.

HURRICANE GLOBE

You will need lavender acrylic paint, paintbrush, 8" dia. wooden plate, preserved skeleton leaves, spray adhesive, waxed paper, 7" dia. paper doily, and a 12"h hurricane globe.

1. Paint plate; allow to dry.

2. Spray wrong sides of leaves with spray adhesive. Use waxed paper to press leaves in place on globe; allow to dry.

3. Place doily, then globe on plate.

PICNIC BASKET

You will need white acrylic paint, paintbrush, picnic basket with hinged lid, tracing paper, batting, fabric, and hot glue.

1. Thin paint with a small amount of water. Lightly paint basket; allow to dry.

2. To make pattern, draw around basket lid on tracing paper; cut out.

3. Use pattern to cut shape from batting. Cut two pieces of fabric $1^{1}/_{2}$" larger on all sides than pattern. For lid lining, cut a piece of cardboard 1" smaller on all sides than pattern.

4. Center batting, then fabric piece on basket lid. Pulling fabric taut and trimming around hinges, glue fabric edges to bottom of lid.

5. For lid liner, center cardboard on wrong side of remaining fabric piece. Pulling fabric taut, glue fabric edges to wrong side of cardboard. Glue wrong side of liner to inside of basket lid.

LAVENDER TOPIARY

You will need a hot glue gun, ⅝" dia. turned wooden knobs, 5"h terra cotta flowerpot, green and white acrylic paint, floral foam, 9" length of wrapping paper tube, dried lavender bunch, preserved galax leaves, white marble chips, and 1½"w wired ribbon.

Refer to Painting Basics, page 127, before beginning project. Allow paint to dry after each application.

1. Glue knobs around rim of pot.

2. Paint pot green. For color wash, mix equal parts of water and white paint; apply to pot. *Spatter Paint* pot with white.

3. Cut floral foam to fit in pot; glue in place. Cut a 3" deep hole in center of foam to fit wrapping paper tube. Place tube in foam; place lavender in tube.

4. Beginning at top and overlapping as needed to cover tube completely, glue leaves to tube.

5. Cover foam surface with marble chips. Tie ribbon into a bow around leaves; notch ribbon ends.

MOSS-COVERED CONSOLE SHELF

You will need a 2¾" x 10½" unfinished wooden shelf, white and green acrylic paint, paintbrushes, wood glue, 12" x 18" piece of cardboard, 2½" dia. foam ball, sheet moss, twigs, freeze-dried gardenia, dried lavender, hot glue gun, and ⅞"w wired ribbon.

Allow paint and glue to dry after each application.

1. Paint shelf and twigs white. Mix equal parts of water and green paint to make a color wash; apply wash over white paint.

2. Referring to Fig. 1, mark, trim, and score cardboard; fold on scored lines. Glue top edge of cardboard to bottom of shelf

Fig. 1

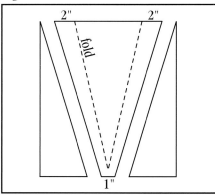

3. Gluing in place, cover front edge of shelf and surface of cardboard with moss.

4. Cut foam ball in half; cover one half with moss.

5. Referring to photo, cut lengths twigs to fit front and side edges of cardboard and shelf; glue in place over moss. Glue moss-covered ball half to bottom of console.

6. Tie ribbon into a bow; notch ends. Glue lavender, gardenia, and bow to center front of console.

OLD FASHIONED HOPE CHEST

You will need a wooden trunk with hinged lid, pre-pasted embossed wallpaper, ⅝"w wooden molding, four fence post caps, hammer and nails, white and green acrylic paint, paintbrushes, batting, fabric, staple gun, 2"w wired ribbon, and a hot glue gun.

Allow paint to dry after each application.

1. Cut wallpaper to fit around outside of trunk; follow manufacturer's instructions to adhere paper to trunk.

2. Cut lengths of molding to fit upper and lower edges of trunk; nail in place. Nail fence post caps to bottom of trunk for feet.

3. Paint trunk white. For color wash, mix equal parts of water and green paint; apply to wallpaper only.

4. Measure width and length of trunk lid; cut a piece of batting the determined measurements. Cut fabric 2" larger on all sides than batting.

5. Center batting, then fabric on trunk lid. Pulling fabric taut and trimming around hinges, bring fabric edges to bottom of lid and staple in place.

6. Cut two lengths of ribbon 4" longer than width of trunk lid. Placing ribbons an equal distance from each end of trunk lid, bring ribbon ends to bottom of lid and staple in place.

7. Tie two bows from ribbon; notch streamer ends. Glue one bow to top front edge of trunk at end of each ribbon piece.

BEDSIDE TABLE

You will need a ready-to-finish wooden table; sandpaper; tack cloth; white primer; white, green, and purple acrylic paint; paintbrushes; and polyurethane sealer.

Refer to Painting Basics, page 127, before beginning project. Allow paint to dry after each application.

1. Sand table; wipe with tack cloth.

2. Apply primer then two coats of white paint to table. Mix equal parts of water and green paint to make a color wash; apply over white paint.

3. Referring to photo, paint simple flower and leaf designs on table.

4. Apply two coats of sealer to table.

PAINTED HEADBOARD

You will need a ready-to-finish wooden headboard; sandpaper; tack cloth; white primer; white; green, and purple acrylic paint; paintbrushes; and polyurethane sealer.

Refer to Painting Basics, page 127, before beginning project. Allow paint to dry after each application.

1. Sand headboard; wipe with tack cloth.

2. Apply primer then two coats of white paint to headboard. Mix equal parts of water and green paint to make a color wash; apply over white paint.

3. Referring to photo, paint simple flower and leaf designs on headboard.

4. Apply two coats of sealer to headboard.

BOLSTER PILLOW

You will need a full-size quilt batting, needle and thread, 3/4 yd. of 54"w fabric, 3/4"w paper-backed fusible web tape, two rubber bands, and 1 1/2 yds. of 1"w wired ribbon.

1. Fold batting lengthwise into thirds. Starting at one end, roll batting tightly to form bolster shape. Stitch edges in place.

2. Following manufacturer's instructions, use tape to fuse a 2"w hem along each edge of fabric piece.

3. Center bolster on one long edge of fabric piece; roll tightly. Gather fabric at each end of bolster and secure with rubber band. Cut ribbon in half; tie each piece into a bow around one end of bolster, covering rubber band. Trim ribbon ends at an angle.

LAVENDER NOSEGAY SCONCES

For each sconce, you will need a 10" square of embossed wallpaper, green acrylic paint, paintbrush, hot glue gun, 3" x 6" piece of cardboard, 1/4" hole punch, 1 yd. of 1"w wired ribbon, and one dried lavender bunch.

1. For color wash, mix equal parts of water and green paint; apply to wallpaper and allow to dry.

2. Referring to Fig. 1, fold and glue wallpaper square to form cone. Fold upper front corner to inside.

Fig. 1

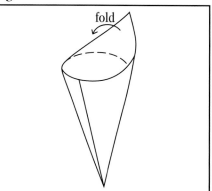

3. Trim one end of cardboard piece to a rounded shape; punch hole in trimmed end. With trimmed end extending above top edge of cone to form hanger, glue cardboard to inside back of sconce over seam.

4. Twist ribbon tightly every 1 1/2" to form scallops. Wrap ribbon around top of sconce, crossing ends at front; glue in place.

5. Place lavender in sconce.

patio
paradise

A PLACE FOR DREAMS TO BLOOM

If your patio doesn't tempt you to sit
and linger, it's time for a makeover. "Open" the door
to this rosy refuge and create a place for dreams to
bloom. The peaceful paradise begins with an artfully
embellished screen door. Plain patio furniture gets
vintage-styling dressed in floral fabrics and lace.
Teamed with etched glassware and garden finds,
candles create a delightful tablescape. A twig sign
declares "The earth laughs in flowers," and a
beautiful floral wreath and hand-painted planter box
prove it. The whimsical teapot birdhouse is an
unexpected pleasure that celebrates
the wonder of nature.

Surveyor's stakes create a picket-fence effect on an old-time screen door. Decorative wooden brackets provide architectural interest and make the door free-standing. A faucet spigot makes a clever door knob, and a brushing of white paint turns the screen into a window of billowy summer clouds.

To enhance the flower-garden setting, slipcover patio chairs (opposite) in ruffled floral fabric with old-fashioned charm.

A simple wooden box (opposite) painted with flowers blends beautifully with the surroundings.

Whimsical touches like our teapot birdhouse, complete with a nest of speckled eggs, and our hand-painted twig sign are delightful little surprises just waiting to be discovered.

The Earth laughs in Flowers

Etched glassware and all-white candles make a lovely table setting. We used a handsome hurricane globe and an ivy bowl, easily embellished with an etching kit. We mounted our glassware atop a vase and pedestals for extra flair.

The romantic beauty of flowers is captured in a grapevine wreath (opposite) abloom with silk roses, hydrangeas, snapdragons, and other naturals from the garden.

patio paradise

CHAIR SEAT AND BACK COVERS

Instructions will make seat and back covers for one chair.

You will need newsprint, fabric, thread, lace trim, 2" thick foam, and an electric knife.

1. For patterns, draw around upper chair back and chair seat on newsprint. Draw a second line $1/2$" outside first on chair back pattern and $1^1/2$" outside first on seat pattern. Cut out patterns on outside lines.

2. Use each pattern to cut two shapes from fabric. Recut seat cushion pattern on inside line. Using electric knife and recut pattern, cut shape from foam.

3. For chair seat ruffles, cut four 9" x 44" pieces from fabric. For chair back ruffles, cut two $3^1/2$" x 44" pieces. Hem both short edges and one long edge of each ruffle by pressing fabric edge $1/4$" to wrong side, $1/4$" to wrong side again and stitching in place. To gather each ruffle, baste $1/4$" and $3/8$" from raw edge. Pull basting threads, gathering one ruffle to fit each edge of seat cushion or each bottom edge of chair back cover.

4. Matching right sides and raw edges, baste one seat ruffle to each edge of one seat fabric shape (ends of ruffles should abut at corners). Placing seat shapes right sides together and leaving a large opening for turning, sew pieces together, enclosing gathered edges of ruffles in seams. Clip corners, turn right side out, insert foam, and sew opening closed.

5. Matching right sides and raw edges, sew one ruffle to bottom edge of each chair back shape. Cut a length of lace trim to fit over each seam; stitch in place. Place both shapes right sides together; stitch $1/2$" from top and side edges. Clip corners and/or curves; turn right side out and press.

ETCHED GLASSWARE WITH CANDLES

You will need assorted clear glass containers for candles (we used a hurricane globe and an ivy bowl); alphabet stencil; clear Con-tact™ paper; craft knife; clean, dry paintbrush; denatured alcohol; unused smooth-textured sponge; and Delta™ PermEnamel White Frost Glass Etching Paint.

1. Wash containers with soapy water; rinse and dry thoroughly.

2. Use fleur-de-lis pattern, page 116, or stencil to draw design on contact paper. Use craft knife to cut out design, leaving surrounding contact paper intact; adhere to container.

3. Follow etching paint manufacturer's instructions to treat area to be etched with alcohol and to etch design on glass.

FLOWER VOTIVES

You will need white acrylic paint, sponge, terra cotta flowerpots, artificial flowers, hot glue gun, glass candlesticks, and votive candles with clear glass holders to fit inside flowerpots.

1. Referring to *Painting Basics*, page 127, sponge paint pots; allow to dry.

2. Remove petals from flowers. Glue petals inside rims of flowerpots and around rims of glass candlesticks.

3. Place votive holders in pots or glue base to top of candlesticks.

TEAPOT BIRDHOUSE

You will need a teapot, drill with ceramic tile drill bit, masking tape, machine oil, household cement, flexible 4" dia. artificial bird's nest, three plastic bird eggs, small artificial fern pick, and 1 yd. of $1^1/2$"w wired ribbon.

1. Referring to Fig. 1 for position, place masking tape over area where hanging hole will be drilled. Lubricating drill bit with oil, drill hole in bottom of teapot; remove tape.

Fig. 1

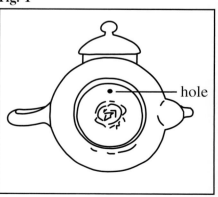

2. Use cement to attach lid to side of teapot (top of birdhouse). Gluing in place, arrange bird's nest, eggs, and fern pick in teapot.

3. Tie ribbon into a bow around knob on teapot lid.

TWIG GARDEN SIGN

You will need a twig arch (we found ours at a craft store), twigs, white and yellow acrylic paint, 3" x 14" flat piece of wood for sign, paintbrushes, black permanent marker, floral wire, hot glue gun, drill and drill bit, and artificial flowers and leaves.

1. Paint arch and twigs white; paint sign yellow. Allow paint to dry.

2. Referring to photo, use black marker to write "The Earth laughs in Flowers" on sign.

3. Cut twigs to fit each edge of sign; glue in place. Drill a hole in each upper corner of sign; use wire to attach sign to bottom of arch.

4. Arrange flowers and leaves on arch and sign and glue in place.

PAINTED PLANTER BOX

You will need a wooden box with hinged lid (we found ours at a flea market); sandpaper; tack cloth; white primer; white, yellow, pink, light blue, blue, and green acrylic paint; paintbrushes; masking tape; screen door handles; and a screwdriver.

Allow paint to dry after each application.

1. Sand wooden box; wipe with tack cloth. Apply primer then two coats of yellow paint to box.

2. Apply strips of masking tape to lid and front of box to form stripes; paint stripes blue. Carefully remove tape. Referring to photo, add simple painted flowers and leaves to front of box.

3. Use screwdriver to attach screen door handles to ends of box and to lid, if desired.

SCREEN DOOR

You will need a screen door (we found ours at a flea market), surveyor's stakes (available at home supply stores), six decorative wooden shelf brackets, faucet head, household cement, hammer and nails, primer, white paint, and paintbrushes.

1. Nail pickets to front of screen door. Position two brackets in upper corners of door frame and nail in place. Placing two on front and two on back, nail remaining brackets to bottom of screen door to hold upright. Use cement to attach faucet head to door for handle.

2. Paint door, including screen, with primer, then with white paint.

SUMMER ROSES WREATH

You will need a large grapevine wreath, artificial silk and dried florals (we used 12 medium roses, 4 large roses, 6 hydrangeas, 3 snapdragons, 12 Queen Anne's lace, 12 maidenhair fern, and three sprigs of purple berries), and a hot glue gun.

1. Arrange roses, snapdragons, and other large items evenly on wreath and glue in place.

2. Glue remaining florals, cut into smaller sections as necessary, in place to fill in remainder of wreath.

garden whimsy

THE PATHWAY TO DELIGHT

If your heart overflows with a passion for the garden, plant an inviting pathway of fanciful yard art. All it takes is a little imagination and some ingenuity. Start with a unique focal point like our whimsical angel. Then scavenge flea markets for old lawn chairs, gates, and other fixtures with flair. Paint them in fresh tints and unify with playful touches like our dragonfly. Sculpt a gardenful of tin-can flowers and add the soothing sound of a water fountain, and you'll reap the rewards of a garden getaway that's truly heavenly!

Posted in the garden atop fancy shelf-bracket feet, this angel (opposite) takes her shape from elements borrowed from the potting shed. Dismantled plastic leaf rakes make her graceful wings, and wooden hand cultivators serve as arms to hold a basket of flowers. A painted flowerpot and saucer form the fashionable skirt, and a coffee-can flower makes a radiant face with bottlecap eyes.

Colorful flowers cut from various-size cans climb a copper tubing "vine" entwined around the pedestal of our paint-splashed birdbath (right).

Friendly painted dragonflies accent these fun concrete stepping stones (below).

Reclaim an old metal laundry tub (opposite) by using it as a garden-side table for storing potting soil. Then you'll have a handy spot to fill creative planters made from everyday castoffs like our rubber boot and kettle.

Cabana stripes and dancing dragonflies freshen a vintage lawn chair, and tin-can flowers and a miniature electric pump turn a metal water can into a flourishing fountain.

Filled with votive candles, prettily painted tin-can luminaries dangle from the tines of a garden rake to welcome guests to the garden. The decorative vine takes shape from medium-gauge wire and leaves cut from aluminum beverage cans. Delight yourself and your backyard guests by painting thoughtful little messages on rocks and scattering them throughout the garden.

For flowers whose beauty will never fade, "plant" giant
blooms fashioned from recycled coffee cans painted in bright colors.

A salvaged chain-link gate abloom with tin-can flowers makes great garden art.

garden whimsy

CONCRETE STEPPING STONES

You will need spray primer; three concrete stepping stones; white, yellow, peach, green, and black acrylic paint; paintbrushes; stencil plastic; craft knife; cutting mat; and clear acrylic spray sealer.

Allow primer, paint, and sealer to dry after each application.

1. Spray each stone with primer, then with desired color paint.

2. Trace dragonfly pattern, page 118, onto stencil plastic; cut out, leaving background intact.

3. Use stencil to paint a dragonfly on each stone. Use black paint to outline dragonfly, paint antennae, detail lines, and eyes. Add white highlights to eyes.

4. Apply two coats of sealer to each stone.

CABANA STRIPED CHAIR

You will need sandpaper; metal patio chair; tack cloth; spray primer; cream and yellow spray paint; white, green, and black acrylic paint; paintbrushes; ³/₄"w painter's masking tape; newspapers; stencil plastic; craft knife; cutting mat; and clear acrylic spray sealer.

Allow primer, paint, and sealer to dry after each application.

1. Sand chair and wipe with tack cloth. Spray chair with primer, then with cream paint.

2. Apply masking tape to back and seat of chair at 2" intervals to form stripes. Cover arms and legs of chair with newspaper to block overspray. Spray paint chair yellow. Remove tape.

3. Trace dragonfly pattern, page 118, onto stencil plastic; cut out, leaving background intact.

4. Use stencil to paint two green dragonflies on chair. Use black paint to outline dragonfly, paint antennae, detail lines, a trailing dashed line, and eyes. Add white highlights to eyes.

5. Apply two coats of sealer to chair.

PAINTED GARDEN ROCKS

You will need rocks; spray primer; cream spray paint; tracing paper; transfer paper; yellow, peach, light green, and green acrylic paint; paintbrushes; and clear acrylic spray sealer.

Allow primer, paint, and sealer to dry after each application.

1. Wash rocks and allow to dry. Spray rocks with primer, then with cream paint.

2. Lightly pencil desired wording on rocks (ours says "Friends are flowers that never fade," "Welcome to my garden," and "Seeds to scatter…dreams to grow"). Trace flower and dragonfly patterns, page 117, onto tracing paper. Use transfer paper to transfer designs to rocks.

3. Paint flowers peach with yellow centers. Paint dragonflies light green. Paint words, outlines, and details green.

4. Apply two coats of sealer to rocks.

GARDEN PLANTERS

You will need a utility knife, rubber boot, spray primer, peach and green spray paint, clear acrylic spray sealer, kettle, hammer, and an awl.

Allow primer, paint, and sealer to dry after each application.

Boot Planter

1. Use utility knife to cut holes in boot for plants.

2. Spray boot with primer, then with two coats of green paint.

3. Apply two coats of sealer to boot.

Kettle Planter

1. Use hammer and awl to punch several drainage holes in bottom of kettle.

2. Spray kettle with primer, then with two coats of peach paint.

3. Apply two coats of sealer to kettle.

HANGING LUMINARIES

You will need three tin vegetable cans; garden rake without handle; drill and bit; utility scissors; five 12-oz. aluminum beverage cans; tracing paper; medium-gauge wire for vines; wire cutters; welding compound; hammer; awl; yellow, peach, blue, green, and dark green spray paint; yellow, peach, blue, and green acrylic paint; paintbrushes; and three votive candles.

Allow primer, paint, and sealer to dry after each application.

1. Fill vegetable cans with water; freeze.

2. Drill a hole through metal ferrule of rake.

3. Use utility scissors to cut through opening and down side of beverage cans; cut away and discard tops and bottoms of cans. Flatten remaining pieces.

4. Trace small leaf pattern, page 117, onto tracing paper; cut out. Use patterns to cut desired number of leaves from can pieces. Fold each leaf in half lengthwise to form crease.

5. Cut two 36" lengths of wire for vines and three 18" lengths for can hangers.

6. Wrap one end of each leaf around vine; following manufacturer's instructions, use welding compound to secure in place. Repeat to attach remaining leaves to vines.

7. For each luminary, remove can from freezer and use hammer and awl to punch holes in can; punch a hole in opposite sides of can 1/2" below rim for hanger. Let ice melt from can; wipe dry.

8. Spray paint ferrule of rake, wire hangers, and vines and leaves green, then spray lightly with light green paint. Spray paint remainder of rake yellow. Spray paint one can yellow, one peach, and one blue. Use acrylic paint to paint desired designs on each can.

9. Thread 6" of one end of one vine through hole in ferrule; form a loop for hanging and twist wire around itself to secure. Curl, twist, and wrap remainder of vine and second vine around upper portion of rake. From outside, thread handle ends into side holes in cans; curl wire ends to secure.

10. Place a candle in each can; hang cans from rake tines.

COFFEE CAN FLOWERS

For each flower, you will need a large coffee can, tin snips, hammer, awl, utility scissors, two 12-oz. aluminum beverage cans, tracing paper, spray primer, 48" length of rebar (available at home supply stores) for stem, green spray paint, desired color of spray paint for flower, assorted colors of acrylic paint, paintbrushes, floral wire, and green vinyl-coated electrical wire.

Wash and dry cans thoroughly. Wear heavy gloves and eye protection while cutting cans. Allow primer, paint, and sealer to dry after each application.

1. For each flower, cut off and discard top rim of can. Cutting to within $1/4$" of bottom rim, cut down sides of can at equal intervals to form petals. Bend petals outward; trim ends to a blunt point.

2. Use hammer and awl to punch two holes in center of flower.

3. Use utility scissors to cut through opening and down side of beverage cans; cut away and discard tops and bottoms of cans. Flatten remaining pieces.

4. Trace large leaf pattern, page 117, onto tracing paper; cut out. Use pattern to cut leaves from can pieces. Fold each leaf in half lengthwise to form crease. Punch two holes in wide end of each leaf.

5. Apply primer to stem, flower, and leaves; paint stem and leaves green. Masking off flower center, spray paint petals desired color. Use acrylic paints to paint dots and lines in center of flower.

6. Use floral wire to attach flower and leaves to stem. For tendrils, form 12" lengths of electrical wire into coils; arrange on stem and wire in place.

TIN CAN FLOWERS

For each flower, you will need tin can (sizes given in instructions), tin snips, acrylic or spray paint (we used white, yellow, blue, green, and peach), paintbrushes, painter's masking tape, clear acrylic spray sealer, hammer, awl, floral wire, and wire cutters.

Wash and dry cans thoroughly. Wear heavy gloves and eye protection while cutting cans. Projects may be painted using acrylic paints or spray painted in sections using masking tape over areas not painted. Allow primer, paint, and sealer to dry after each application.

Blue Flowers

1. Use a 2"h x $3^1/4$" dia. can. For petals, cut can from top edge to bottom at $1^1/4$" intervals. Bend petals outward.

2. Apply primer to flower. Paint petals blue and center of flower yellow. Paint thin blue crisscrossed lines on center.

3. Punch two small holes at center of flower. Use wire to attach flower to project.

Yellow Flowers

1. Use a $1^1/2$"h x 3" dia. can. For petals, cut can from top edge to bottom at $1^1/4$" intervals. Bend petals outward; trim ends into a rounded shape.

2. Apply primer to flower. Paint petals yellow and center white. Paint a blue swirl design and yellow dots on center.

3. Punch two small holes at center of flower. Use wire to attach flower to project.

Green Flowers

1. Use a vegetable can. For petals, cut can from top edge to bottom at $3/4$" intervals. Bend petals outward; trim ends to a blunt point.

2. Apply primer to flower. Paint petals green and center white. Paint peach dots on center.

3. Punch two holes at center of flower. Use wire to attach flower to project.

Peach Flowers

1. Use two vegetable cans (one should fit inside the other). For petals, cut small can from top edge to bottom at $3/4$" intervals; cut larger can at $1^1/4$" intervals. Bend petals outward.

2. Apply primer to flowers. Paint petals peach and centers white. Paint peach dots and green lines on center of smaller can.

3. Punch two holes at center of each flower. Positioning small flower over larger flower, use wire to attach to project.

Leaves

1. Use utility scissors to cut through opening and down side of beverage cans; cut away and discard tops and bottoms of cans. Flatten remaining pieces.

2. Trace large leaf pattern, page 117, onto tracing paper; cut out. Use pattern to cut leaves from can pieces. Fold each leaf lengthwise to form center crease.

3. Spray leaves with primer, then with green paint.

4. Punch two holes in wide end of each leaf; use wire to attach leaf to project.

FLOWERED GARDEN GATE

You will need steel wool, chain link garden gate, spray primer, cream spray paint, green acrylic paint, paintbrush, $1/4$" dia. copper tubing, assorted *Tin Can Flowers,* and green vinyl-coated electrical wire.

Allow primer and paint to dry after each application.

1. Use steel wool to clean gate. Wash gate and allow to dry. Spray gate with primer, then with cream paint. Paint scrollwork at top of gate green.

2. Threading copper tubing for vine through chain link, arrange on gate as desired.

3. Arrange flowers and leaves on vine and wire in place. For tendrils, form 12" lengths of electrical wire into a coil; arrange on vine and wire in place.

FLOWERED BIRDBATH

You will need birdbath, $1/4$" dia. copper tubing, assorted *Tin Can Flowers,* and green vinyl-coated electrical wire.

1. Arrange copper tubing (vine) around base of birdbath as desired.

2. Arrange flowers and leaves on vine and wire in place.

3. For tendrils, form 12" lengths of electrical wire into coils; arrange on vine and wire in place.

POTTING TABLE

You will need steel wool; metal laundry tub (we found ours at a flea market); spray primer; cream, yellow, and green spray paint; stencil plastic; white and black acrylic paint; paintbrushes; $1/2$" dia. copper tubing; assorted *Tin Can Flowers,* green vinyl-coated electrical wire; wire cutters; floral wire; $1/2$" plywood; 1" x 2" furrier strip; $1^1/2$" long nails; $1/2$" thick quarter-round molding; 1"w painter's masking tape; and clear acrylic spray sealer.

Allow primer, paint, and sealer to dry after each application.

1. Use steel wool to clean tub surface. Wash tub and allow to dry. Spray tub with primer, then with green paint.

2. Trace dragonfly pattern, page 118, onto stencil plastic; cut out, leaving background intact. Use stencil and acrylic paint to paint yellow dragonflies on tub. Use black paint to outline dragonflies, paint antennae, detail lines, a trailing dashed line, and eyes. Add white highlights to eyes. Apply two coats of sealer to tub.

3. Wrap copper tubing around base of tub to form vine. Arrange flowers and leaves as desired on vine, using floral wire to secure. For tendrils, form 12" lengths of electrical wire into coils; arrange on vine and wire in place.

4. For potting table lid, measure length and width of tub; add 4" to each measurement. Cut a piece of plywood the determined size. On wrong side of lid; draw a line 2" in from each edge. Cutting to fit, nail lengths of furrier strip along inner edge of drawn line.

5. Cutting to fit and mitering at corners, attach lengths of molding to edges of lid with small nails.

6. Spray lid with primer, then with cream paint. Use masking tape to mask off stripes at 2" intervals. Paint lid yellow. Remove masking tape. Apply two coats of sealer to lid.

WATER CAN FOUNTAIN

You will need a 5-gallon insulated metal water can (we found ours at a flea market), steel wool, spray primer, yellow spray paint, $1/4$" dia. copper tubing, assorted *Tin Can Flowers,* floral wire, wire cutters, green vinyl-coated electrical wire, two 6" dia. clay flowerpots, clay saucer to fit over top of one flowerpot, fountain pump with plastic tubing, fountain spray nozzle, and duct tape.

Allow primer and paint to dry after each application.

1. Use steel wool to clean water can. Wash can and allow to dry. Spray can with primer, then with yellow paint.

2. Arrange copper tubing through handles and across front of can to form vine.

3. Use wire to attach flowers and leaves to vine. For tendrils, form 12" lengths of electrical wire into coils; arrange on vine and wire in place.

4. To raise pump to correct height inside water can, place first clay pot upside down in can, place saucer on first clay pot, and place second clay pot upside down on saucer. Place pump on top pot. Cut 2" from plastic tubing; place one end of tubing on pump and opposite end on nozzle. Secure clay pots, pump, and plastic tubing in place with duct tape.

5. Follow pump manufacturer's instructions to add water and start pump.

GARDEN ANGEL

You will need electric drill and bit set; saw; four 8¹/₂" x 13¹/₂" decorative wooden shelf brackets; wood glue; 8' long 4" x 4" wooden post; ³/₄" long #6 flat-head wood screws; spray primer; cream, yellow, peach, and green spray paint; 13¹/₂" dia. plastic flowerpot saucer; 16" dia. polystyrene flowerpot; hammer; 2" long nails; 1" x 2" furrier strip; two furniture clamps; 4" long #12 flat-head wood screws; two 18" lengths of 2" x 2" lumber for arms; two hand cultivators without handles; 1" dia. washers; two plastic leaf rakes without handles; large coffee can; tin snips; masking tape; 12-oz. aluminum beverage can; tracing paper; two metal bottle caps; yellow and blue acrylic paint; paintbrushes; household cement; clear spray sealer; 1 yd. of 2"w grosgrain ribbon; 14" long rectangular basket with handles; and plants for basket.

Allow cement, wood glue, primer, paint, and sealer to dry after each application. Refer to Assembly Diagram, page 115, to assemble Garden Angel. Use drill and ¹/₃₂" bit to make pilot holes for screws.

1. Referring to Fig. 1, cut 4" x 4" post to make one body post and two torso pieces.

Fig. 1

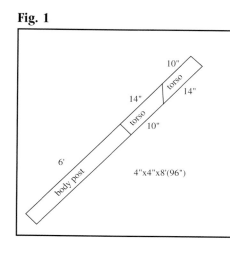

2. For angel base, use wood glue to glue one wooden bracket at center bottom of each side of body post; allow to dry. Insert three #6 wood screws into each bracket to secure to post. Cut four 3¹/₂" lengths from furrier strip; nail pieces around post 33" from bottom.

3. Spray body post and base, torso pieces, arms, and flowerpot with primer. Paint upper 3' of post, torso pieces, arms, and flowerpot peach. Masking off upper part of post, spray paint base and bottom 3' of post green.

4. For skirt, cut 4" square openings in center bottom of saucer and flowerpot. Place saucer inside flowerpot and cement in place. Slide skirt onto post until it rests on furrier strip pieces. Cement edges of skirt to post at each opening to secure.

5. With long sides of torso pieces on opposite sides of post, use wood glue to glue torso pieces in place 6" below top of post. Apply furniture clamps to hold pieces in place while glue dries. For brace, use #6 screws to attach a 9" length from furrier strip across back of torso. Insert a #12 screw at an angle through lower end of each torso piece into post.

6. For hands, drill one hole in one end of each arm and insert shaft of cultivator. With two washers between arm and torso, use one #12 screw to attach one arm to each shoulder.

7. For wings, use #12 screws and washers to secure leaf rakes to back of angel.

8. For flower face, follow Step 1 of *Coffee Can Flowers*, page 112, to make flower. Spray flower with primer, then with cream paint. Mask off center of head and paint petals yellow.

9. Use utility scissors to cut through opening and down side of beverage can; cut away and discard top and bottom of can. Flatten remaining piece. Trace flower pattern, page 118, onto tracing paper; cut out. Draw around pattern twice on can piece; cut out. Apply primer to flowers and bottle caps. Paint flowers yellow and bottle caps blue. To assemble each eye, center one bottle cap on each flower; cement in place. Position eyes on face and cement in place. Apply two to three coats of sealer to face.

10. Use a #6 screw at top and bottom of face to secure to top of post. Spray paint heads of screws with cream paint.

11. Tie ribbon into a bow around angel's waist; trim and notch ribbon ends. Place basket in hands; place plants in basket.

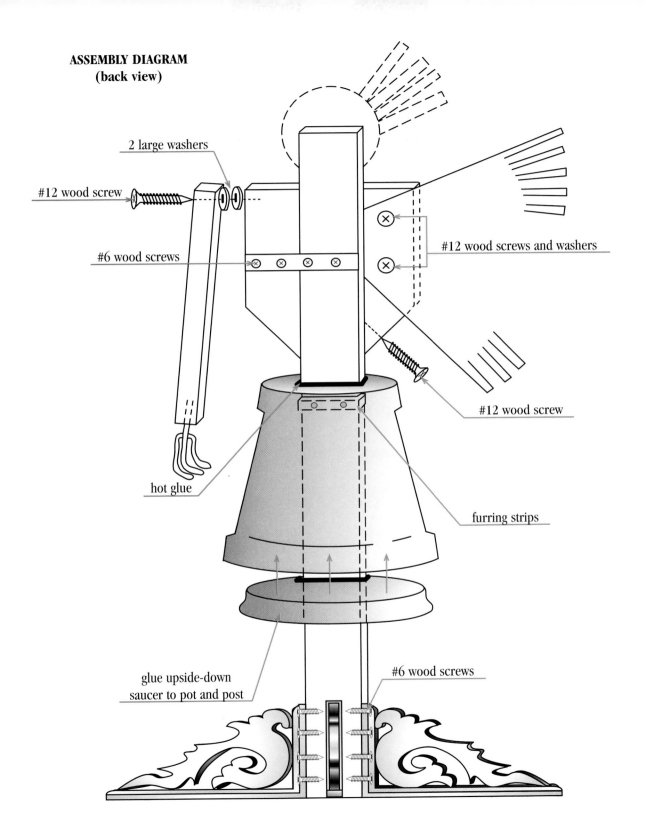

ASSEMBLY DIAGRAM
(back view)

2 large washers

#12 wood screw

#6 wood screws

#12 wood screws and washers

#12 wood screw

hot glue

furring strips

glue upside-down
saucer to pot and post

#6 wood screws

Patterns

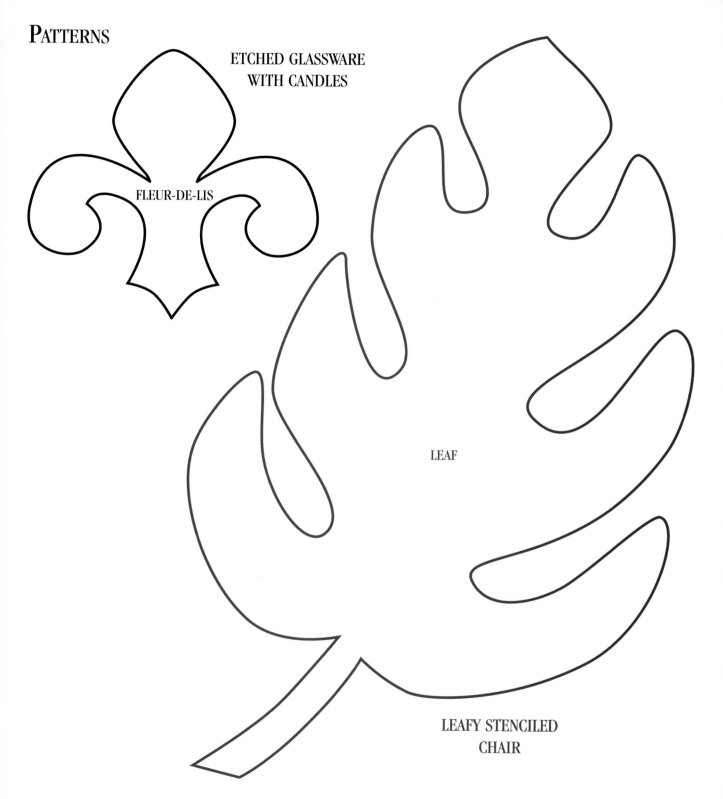

ETCHED GLASSWARE
WITH CANDLES

FLEUR-DE-LIS

LEAF

LEAFY STENCILED
CHAIR

PAINTED GARDEN ROCKS

SMALL
DRAGONFLY

FLOWERS

PAINTED ROCKING
CHAIR

FLOWERPOT

SMALL
LEAF

HANGING
LUMINARIES

LARGE
LEAF

COFFEE CAN FLOWERS
TIN CAN FLOWERS

117

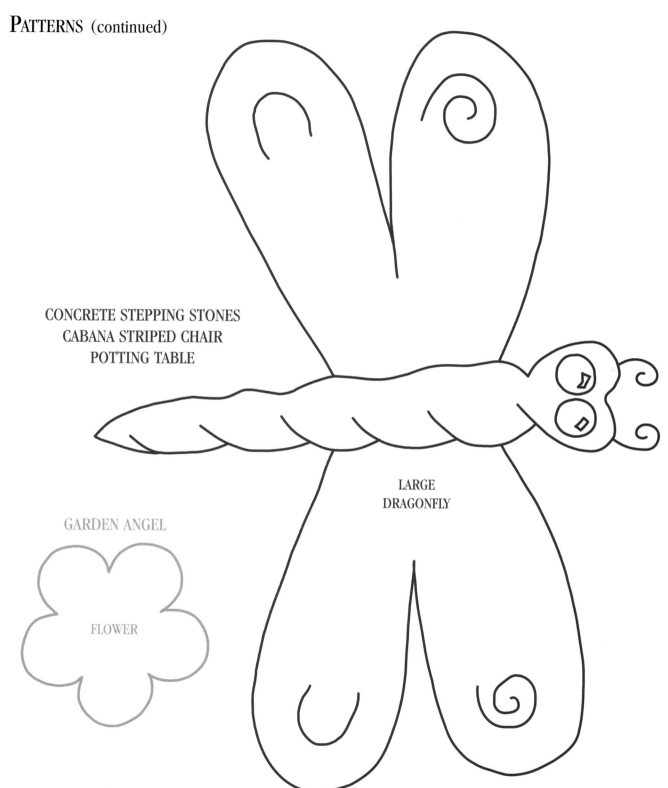

CONCRETE STEPPING STONES
CABANA STRIPED CHAIR
POTTING TABLE

LARGE
DRAGONFLY

GARDEN ANGEL

FLOWER

Reproduced from this book or otherwise transmitted, but is licensed for use only. Copied for personal use only, granted permission to photocopy this page for personal use only.

119

ORANGER À LONGUES FEUILLES

Arancio à foglia lunga

Tab 21

Poiteau Pinx.^t

Thé. Susemihl Sculp.^t

ORANGER DE GÈNES,
Arancio di Genova,
Tab. 8.

Poiteau Pinx.   Gabriel Sculp.

Leisure Arts, Inc., grants permission to the owner of this book to photocopy this page for personal use only. Enlarge 157%.

121

LIMONIER BIGNETTE.

Limone Bignetta.

Tab. 73.

Poiteau pinx.   *Gabriel sculp.*

Leisure Arts, Inc., grants permission to the owner of this book to photocopy this page for personal use only. Enlarge 15%.

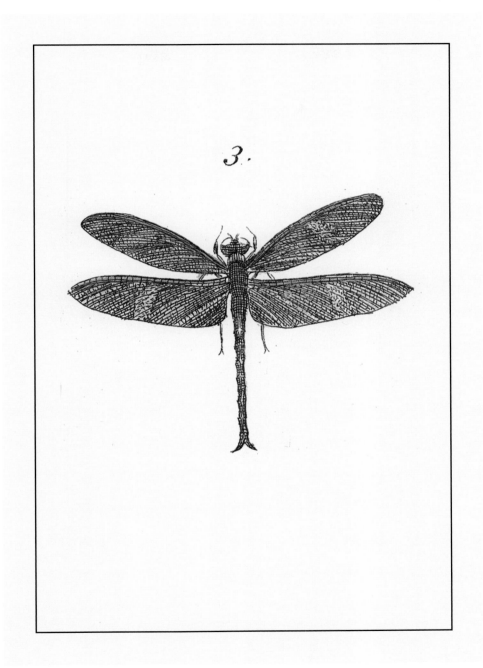

3.

Leisure Arts, Inc., grants permission to
the owner of this book to photocopy this
page for personal use only.

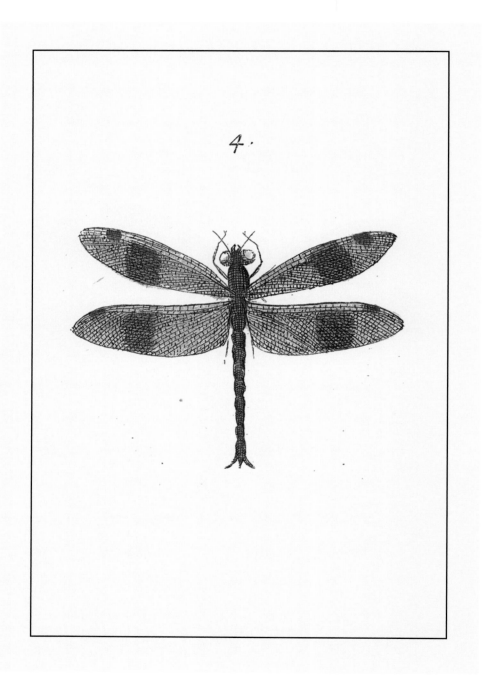

*Leisure Arts, Inc., grants permission to
the owner of this book to photocopy this
page for personal use only.*

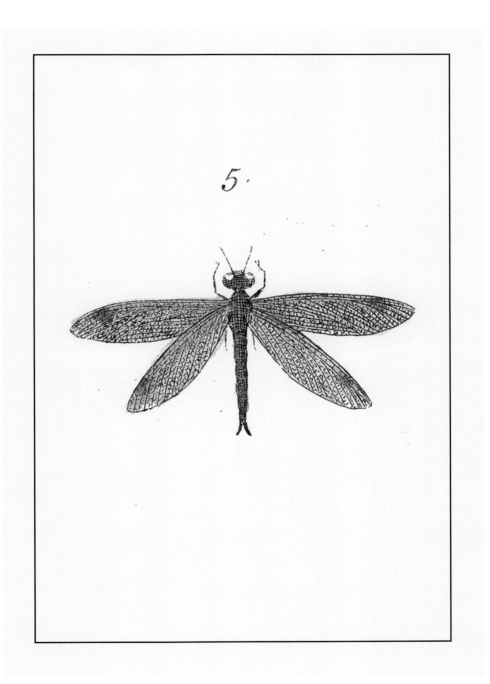

5.

*Leisure Arts, Inc., grants permission to
the owner of this book to photocopy this
page for personal use only.*

6.

*Leisure Arts, Inc., grants permission to
the owner of this book to photocopy this
page for personal use only.*

GENERAL INSTRUCTIONS

PAINTING BASICS

To achieve the desired results, practice these decorative painting basics before beginning your project.

Transferring a pattern: Trace pattern onto tracing paper. Place transfer paper coated side down between project and traced pattern. Use removable tape to secure pattern to project. Use a stylus to transfer outlines of design to project (press lightly to avoid smudges and heavy lines that are difficult to cover). If necessary, use a soft eraser to remove any smudges.

Basecoating: Dip flat paintbrush in water; dip in paint. Apply thin coat of paint to surface, smoothing with wet paint to prevent any ridges; let dry.

Dry Brushing: Do not dip brush in water. Dip brush in paint; wipe most of the paint off onto a dry paper towel. Lightly rub the brush in a circular motion, starting in the center of the area to receive color. Decrease pressure on the brush as you move outward. Repeat as needed.

Lining: For most lining, use 18/0 or 10/0 liner brush. Thin paint to an ink-like consistency. Dip brush in water; blot on paper towel. Load brush by placing bristles in paint and dragging away from puddle to get a pointed tip. Hold brush perpendicular to surface, about 1" above ferrule. Place tip on surface and pull brush toward you. Pull from your elbow, not from your wrist. When paint begins skipping, reload brush and begin again, backing up a little from where you ended to keep line the same width.

Stenciling: To make stencil, cut a piece of vinyl template material at least 1" larger on all sides than pattern. Place template material directly over pattern in book. Use a fine point permanent marker to trace pattern. Place template material on cutting mat and use craft knife to cut out design sections, making sure edges are smooth.

Pour a small amount of paint onto a paper plate. Hold or tape (using removable tape) stencil in place on project. Dip a stencil brush or sponge piece in paint and remove excess on a paper towel. Working from edges of cut-out areas toward center, apply paint in a stamping motion. Carefully lift stencil from project. To stencil a design in reverse, clean stencil and turn stencil over.

Spatter painting: Dip the bristle tips of a toothbrush into paint, blot on paper towel to remove excess, then pull thumb across bristles to spatter paint on project.

Sponge painting: Pour a small amount of paint onto a paper plate. Dip dampened sponge piece into paint and remove excess on a paper towel. Use a light stamping motion to apply paint. Reapply paint to sponge as necessary.

RUNNING STITCH

Referring to Fig. 1, make a series of straight stitches with stitch length equal to the space between stitches.

Fig. 1

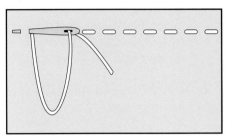

CUTTING A FABRIC CIRCLE

Matching right sides, fold fabric square in half from top to bottom and again from left to right.

Refer to project instructions for diameter of fabric circle; determine radius of circle by dividing diameter in half. Tie one end of string to fabric marking pencil. Insert thumbtack through string and fabric as show in Fig. 1 and mark cutting line. Cut along drawn line through all fabric layers. Unfold circle.

Fig. 1

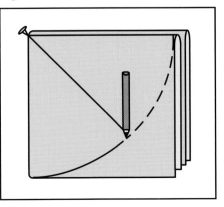

CREDITS

We want to extend a warm *thank you* to the generous people who allowed us to photograph our projects at their homes:

Inviting Retreat and *Airy Living Room:* John and Anne Jarrard
Delightful Den: The Mansion Art Centre
Sunny Breakfast Room: Tim and Janna Laughlin
Zesty Dining Room and *Home Office Haven:* Molly Satterfield
Refreshing Bedroom: Dan and Sandra Cook
Patio Paradise: Richard and Lange Cheek
Garden Whimsy: Duncan and Nancy Porter

To Wisconsin Technicolor LLC of Pewaukee, Wisconsin, we say *thank you* for the superb color reproduction and excellent pre-press preparation.

We want to especially thank photographers Ken West of Peerless Photography, Little Rock, Arkansas, and Jerry R. Davis of Jerry Davis Photography, Little Rock, Arkansas, for their excellent work.

We also want to thank Black Ink, Inc., for providing the preserved skeleton leaves used in the *Refreshing Bedroom* and *Home Office Haven* sections.

The prints used in the *Zesty Dining Room* and *Home Office Haven* sections were taken from *COLLECTIONS: CLASSIC PRINTS FOR TODAY'S HOME,* published by Riverwood Press for Leisure Arts.